T0356266

Praise for *The Capitalist and the Activist*

"Engrossing book . . . A well-researched, absorbing, and balanced case for corporate-activist partnerships."
—*Kirkus Reviews*

"There simply couldn't be a more timely and instructive treatment of the melding of the traditions of corporate capitalism with the spirit of social activism. Employing compelling narratives and arguments, Lin ushers us into a stunning recognition of the implications of this vitally important fusion for our political future."
—**Robert Cialdini, *New York Times* bestselling author of *Influence* and *Pre-Suasion***

"Filled with insight. *The Capitalist and the Activist* is essential reading for anyone trying to understand and navigate this era of profound change in business and society. Through well-crafted narratives and thought-provoking analysis, Tom Lin reveals the larger forces influencing the decisions of executives, politicians, and citizens."
—**Jonah Berger, *New York Times* bestselling author of *Contagious* and *The Catalyst***

"Should corporations use their power to influence politics? Should warriors for racial, gender, and environmental justice treat corporations as foes or as sources of effective strategies? Have corporations become a vital check and balance given out-of-control or paralyzed politicians? With vivid stories and sensible analysis, Tom Lin traces the emergence of new border crossings between American money-making and social-change-making enterprises. Offering a striking perspective on our times, this book provides wise principles to navigate the shifting borders of public, private, politics, and profits."
—**Martha Minow, former Dean, Harvard Law School, and author of *Partners, Not Rivals***

"If the promise of our nation's highest ideals is to be better realized, we must have a business community that recognizes that companies succeed only because of their workers, the communities in which they operate, and the support that taxpayers provide in so many ways, direct and indirect. Professor Lin's provocative and timely new book spells out a road map for business leaders to follow if they truly want to create sustainably profitable businesses that treat all their stakeholders well."
—**The Honorable Leo E. Strine, Jr., former Chief Justice of the Delaware Supreme Court**

"*The Capitalist and the Activist* is an invaluable read for business executives, investors, entrepreneurs, and anyone trying to understand contemporary business and social activism. With wonderfully written analysis and compelling stories, Tom Lin masterfully examines and explains the new fault lines of business, politics, and activism."

—Lawrence A. Cunningham, bestselling author of *The Essays of Warren Buffett* and *Berkshire beyond Buffett*

"Corporate management and boards must consider the interests not only of shareholders but also of employees, customers, suppliers, communities, the environment, and other constituencies that are critical to the long-term sustainable success of the corporation. The pursuit of wealth maximization for shareholders as the sole purpose of corporate governance has been a principal accelerant of short-termism and socioeconomic inequality that is undermining our constitutional democracy. This timely book gives insight into the problems and the avenues for redress through an engaging discussion of modern stakeholder governance."

—Martin Lipton, a founding partner of Wachtell, Lipton, Rosen & Katz

"Lin has written a nuanced, thoughtful, and thorough book about the most important issue in corporate law right now: do corporations have social responsibilities and how effective are corporate initiatives that attempt to confront the most vexing social issues? This book is a must-read for policymakers, corporate managers, and citizens who want an unbiased and accurate discussion of the law and the state of play. Lin uses case studies of recent campaigns by corporations who have mobilized to confront wide-scale social movements like Black Lives Matter, #metoo, climate justice, and voting rights. This is an important book that makes for a riveting and enlightening read."

—Mehrsa Baradaran, author of *The Color of Money* and *How The Other Half Banks*

"This is an ambitious and uplifting book. In a world that is plagued with injustice, racism, inequity, and inequality, Tom Lin lucidly lays out why and how activists and corporations can work together to fulfill our collective moral obligations to our communities and our planet. *The Capitalist and the Activist* shows us that we can seek social as well as financial returns to benefit humanity. It is brimming with hope and insight and is an affirmation of all those who already collaborate."

—Sister Nora M. Nash, Director, Corporate Social Responsibility, Sisters of St. Francis of Philadelphia

"Tom Lin mixes analysis and inspiration to light a pathway forward for stakeholders inside and outside the corporate world who want the engines of capitalism to help drive sustainable social reform."

—Donald Langevoort, Thomas Aquinas Reynolds Professor of Law, Georgetown University

THE

CAPITALIST

AND THE

ACTIVIST

THE
CAPITALIST
AND THE
ACTIVIST

CORPORATE SOCIAL ACTIVISM AND
THE NEW BUSINESS OF CHANGE

TOM C.W. LIN

BK

Berrett–Koehler Publishers, Inc.

Berrett-Koehler Publishers, Inc.
1333 Broadway, Suite 1000
Oakland, CA 94612-1921
Tel: (510) 817-2277
Fax: (510) 817-2278
www.bkconnection.com

ORDERING INFORMATION

Quantity sales. Special discounts are available on quantity purchases by corporations, associations, and others. For details, contact the "Special Sales Department" at the Berrett-Koehler address above.

Individual sales. Berrett-Koehler publications are available through most bookstores. They can also be ordered directly from Berrett-Koehler: Tel: (800) 929-2929; Fax: (802) 864-7626; www.bkconnection.com.

Orders for college textbook / course adoption use. Please contact Berrett-Koehler: Tel: (800) 929-2929; Fax: (802) 864-7626.

Distributed to the U.S. trade and internationally by Penguin Random House Publisher Services.

Berrett-Koehler and the BK logo are registered trademarks of Berrett-Koehler Publishers, Inc.

Printed in Canada

Berrett-Koehler books are printed on long-lasting acid-free paper. When it is available, we choose paper that has been manufactured by environmentally responsible processes. These may include using trees grown in sustainable forests, incorporating recycled paper, minimizing chlorine in bleaching, or recycling the energy produced at the paper mill.

Library of Congress Cataloging-in-Publication Data

Names: Lin, Tom C.W., author.

Title: The capitalist and the activist : corporate social activism and the new business of change / Tom C.W. Lin.
Description: Oakland, CA : Berrett-Koehler Publishers, 2022. | Includes bibliographical references and index.
Identifiers: LCCN 2021033459 (print) | LCCN 2021033460 (ebook) | ISBN 9781523091997 (hardcover ; alk. paper) | ISBN 9781523092000 (adobe pdf) | ISBN 9781523092550 (epub)
Subjects: LCSH: Corporations--Political activity. | Business and politics. | Social responsibility of business. | Capitalism--Social aspects. | Social change.
Classification: LCC HD2326 .L526 2022 (print) | LCC HD2326 (ebook) | DDC 322/.3--dc23
LC record available at https://lccn.loc.gov/2021033459
LC ebook record available at https://lccn.loc.gov/20210334600

First Edition
28 27 26 25 24 23 22   10 9 8 7 6 5 4 3 2 1

Book production and design: Seventeenth Street Studios
Cover designer: Tom C.W. Lin, Nicole Hayward

For my family, near and far.

CONTENTS

WE ARE A TRIBAL SPECIES. Unlike young schoolchildren, we prefer division to addition. We divide ourselves into groups of our own justification, sensible or not. Hunters or gatherers. Settlers or nomads. Men or women. Cis or trans. Natives or immigrants. Citizens or noncitizens. Black or White. Rich or poor. Gay or straight. Believers or nonbelievers. Extroverts or introverts. Rural or urban. Nationalists or globalists. Republican or Democrat. Conservative or progressive.

We prefer our tribes to the others. We believe in the superiority of our tribe, and we push back against those who threaten our group. Our tribes give us a sense of belonging, cooperation, purpose, comfort, and support. We nurture our tribes with myths and morals, facts and fictions, to bind ourselves to one another.

Yet these ties that bind us can also blind us. They can blind us to our limited imagination, to our prejudices, to our similarities, to our shared humanity, to our common hopes, and to our greater good.

This book is in one sense about two dominant tribes in modern life: the capitalists and the activists. It is about those who seek to change the world through the private market forces of business, commerce, and entrepreneurialism, and those who seek to change the world through the public social forces of protest, movement, and organization. It is a book about an unexpected and uneasy coming together of these two tribes, of capitalists and activists, to change our lives and our society during an era when the world seems to be coming apart.

In recent years, crisis after crisis has bruised, battered, and barricaded the United States and the world. An unforgiving, deadly virus circumnavigated the globe, massive wildfires seared thousands of acres of homeland, record rainstorms flooded entire countries, and an inhumane racism reared its hateful face again and again. Stores shuttered. People starved. Homes burned. Cities emptied. Crime rose. Jobs lost. Families destroyed. And too many lives ended too soon.

During these uncertain and tumultuous times, many people have retreated into dangerous impulses of tribalism, seeking to blame and hurt others for painful changes they have experienced, reviving ancient grievances for a new generation, denying reality to fit their convenient tribal myths, insurrecting against popular will to violently reclaim lost power.

Old divisions—buried and ignored for too long—have manifested cruelly and bleakly, reminding us of a harsh history that is still ever present and never really past. A normal state of injustice and struggle for some has become self-evident for all seeking a new sense of normal.

Yet during this dark period streams of bright light have come from activists and capitalists.

The righteous, do-better spirit of activists blossomed from the soils of injustice. Moved by the wrongs they witnessed from the safety of their quarantined homes, masses of activists of every creed, color, and age risked their lives and health to peacefully march, stand, and kneel for justice across the country. Battered by hurricanes, singed by wildfires, scorched by heat waves, drowned by unforgiving floods, and frozen by blizzards, activists marched and lobbied for a greener, more sustainable future. Galvanized by an urgency for change, activists in the United States organized millions to vote and engage in the political process.

Similarly, the entrepreneurial, can-do spirit of many good capitalists has persisted in the depths of a pandemic, across acres of flames and valleys of systemic wrongs. Motivated by the activists, businesses gave hundreds of millions of hours and dollars to fight racial injustice. Propelled by the constraints and failings of our public institutions and leaders, numerous companies provided necessities to help local communities. Animated by memories of the dead and dying, scientists and executives at pharmaceutical companies worked tirelessly to discover and distribute cures for a deadly virus.

Too often the stories of activists and capitalists are told as disparate, unrelated stories of distinct tribes in their own languages: one as a story of selfless acts for the public good, and the other as a story of selfish pursuit for private profit. These narratives suggest that those working in private enterprise have little to do with those toiling in public service, and vice versa.

Telling and understanding these stories as separate tales belies the fact that within all of us are impulses to act in support of causes for the public good as well as desires for personal gain; that within all of us are both capitalists and activists. Telling and understanding these stories as separate tales also obscures potentially powerful lessons and principles that we can derive and use to create something better. For the truth of the matter is that more and more these stories of activism and capitalism are part of one larger story.

The Capitalist and the Activist tells this one greater unfolding story about business, social change, and progress in contemporary America. This book tells this larger story in a simple but not oversimplified manner, to bring more people into conversations and discussions that have been happening in the rarefied cloisters of boardrooms, classrooms, and conference rooms. It tells this larger story during a period when old assumptions, old biases, old ways, and old narratives are being challenged and changed. It tells this larger story mindful of the structural shortcomings and systemic limitations of capitalism and activism, yet optimistic of the possibilities of progress. It tells this larger story to business executives, astute investors, community activists, engaged citizens, interested scholars, inquisitive students, and all those curious to understand the forces shaping the social changes unfolding around them.

This book aspires to remind us about the roads we have traveled for progress, and the roads we can construct to overcome obstacles, old and new, toward something better using the means of capitalism and activism. Understandably, no single book—and certainly not this one—can contain all or even most of the solutions to the social problems that have plagued us for so long. But a book can help us understand how we arrived here, how we can see things differently, and how we can change. It can give us a shared framework, a common tribal story to motivate us, to push ahead, to move forward.

The Irish poet Seamus Heaney once said, "If you have the words, there's always a chance that you'll find the way."[1] Ultimately, *The Capitalist and the Activist* is an attempt to put into words the larger story of activism, capitalism, and social change unfolding around us. It is a hopeful story of promises and perils. It is a story that we all share and can all shape together to help us find the way—the way forward toward rebuilding anew something extraordinarily better.

Here is that story.

INTRODUCTION

Reimagining Capitalism and Activism

I T WAS VALENTINE'S DAY, and hearts were going to be irrepara-
bly broken. On a sunny Wednesday, February 14, 2018, a
nineteen-year-old gunman walked into Marjory Stoneman
Douglas High School in Parkland, Florida, and opened fire on
students, faculty, and staff. In the span of about ten minutes,
seventeen people were killed, fourteen of them teenagers, and
countless lives and families were broken.

In the aftermath, the response from the public and the politicians echoed those of many other mass shootings since the massacre at Columbine High School in Colorado nearly two decades
earlier. A shocked nation and a shattered community grieved
unimaginable loss while politicians offered thoughts and prayers
and vows to never again let such tragedies occur. Yet time and

time again since the Columbine shooting in 1999, mass shootings would occur and so would the same rhetoric without any meaningful action.

Parkland would be different. In the aftermath of the Parkland shooting, surviving students at Marjory Stoneman Douglas organized using traditional and social media to raise awareness and action to curb gun violence in America. Merely a month after the shooting, on Wednesday, March 14, 2018, nearly a million students walked out of their classrooms for the National School Walkout.

Within the span of a few weeks, the students remarkably translated their activism into real results, despite strong resistance from powerful political forces like the National Rifle Association (NRA). The state of Florida, which has one of the most strident pro-gun political establishments, enacted laws that raised the age for purchasing firearms, implemented background checks with waiting periods, outlawed certain gun accessories like bump stocks, and prohibited gun ownership from certain segments of the population.

The activism of the students also led to an unprecedented global demonstration, with over one million participants, known as the March for Our Lives on Saturday, March 24, 2018, in Washington, DC, and numerous cities around the country and the world. This overwhelming wave of activism ultimately led to more scrutiny of the NRA, which resulted in the organization filing for bankruptcy in 2021 to circumvent investigations from the New York state attorney general.

Incredibly, four high school students along with their classmates moved over a million people and the powers that be to take action in ways that others, much older and better resourced, could not—and had not for decades.

The response to Parkland was different not just because of the remarkable activism of the students, but also because of the response from corporate America. The newly animated activism surrounding gun violence moved some of the largest and most profitable corporations in the world to act on the politically fraught issue of guns in America. Dick's Sporting Goods, the country's largest sporting goods retailer and one of the nation's largest gun vendors, announced that it would immediately end sales of all assault-style rifles and high-capacity magazines and raise the gun-buying age to twenty-one. Walmart, the nation's largest retailer and gun seller, raised the age restriction for the purchase of firearms and ammunition to twenty-one and removed items that resembled assault-style rifles, including toy guns, from its website.

More surprisingly, companies whose businesses did not directly involve guns and ammunitions also took action. Citigroup restricted its banking clients from offering bump stocks and high-capacity magazines and required them to institute background checks and a twenty-one-year-old minimum age requirement for any firearm purchase.[1] Citigroup's new policies applied broadly to clients, including those who used its credit cards, borrowed money, or raised capital through the company. Similarly, Bank of America issued an institutional prohibition for loans to gun manufacturers that make military-inspired firearms for civilian use, like the AR-15-style rifles used in the Parkland shooting and other mass shootings.[2] Furthermore, spurred by the "#BoycottNRA" movement that trended on Twitter after the shooting, corporations such as United Airlines, Delta Airlines, Hertz, and Avis announced that they would no longer offer discount programs for the NRA's five million members.[3]

While the ultimate, long-term political and social impact of the activism following Parkland remains to be seen, the actions of the students and businesses highlight the changing reality of social activism and social change in contemporary America. To be sure, they did not and will not eradicate all mass gun violence in the United States, but expediency and perfection have never been the metrics of success for any meaningful social progress. Rather, more importantly, the activism that followed Parkland offers glimmers of hope for some of the toughest social challenges, through leveraging the powers of capitalism and activism during a period of partisan gridlock and political dysfunction in government.

THE NEW REALITY OF CAPITALISM AND ACTIVISM

The days when activists focused on moral fights over social issues while businesses concentrated on the amoral pursuit of commercial profit are gone. Today, businesses and their executives are at the frontlines of some of the most contentious and important social issues of our time. Through pronouncements, policies, boycotts, sponsorships, lobbying, and fundraising, corporations are actively and publicly engaged in issues like voting rights, racial justice, income inequality, gun violence, immigration reform, gender equality, and climate change. This is the new reality of capitalism and activism in America.

This book is about this complicated new reality of corporate social activism in American life, the consequential interplay between capitalists and activists on some of the most pressing issues of our time, and the implications for our businesses and our lives. Weaving studies and stories, this book is an attempt to understand how we arrived at this moment—in which activists and capitalists often join forces to address some of society's most difficult challenges—and what it means for our future. It examines how the definitions of activist and capitalist have blurred in our times. It explores how we arrived here and where we are going as a nation of capitalists and activists seeking profits and progress.

THE ROOTS OF THE NEW CORPORATE SOCIAL ACTIVISM

This book unfolds over the course of ten chapters. It begins by revealing how three larger, interconnected developments in business, law, and society gave rise to the new corporate social activism. Specifically, the first three chapters explain how the evolution of corporate purpose, the convergence of the public and private sectors, and the expansion of corporate political rights all helped foster a fusion of capitalism and activism that is at the heart of contemporary social change.

Chapter 1 explores the evolution of corporate purpose in America from an understanding of businesses as amoral engines of profit to socially responsible vehicles of profit *and* social progress. Using the fundamental debates in law and public policy surrounding the seminal works and ideas of Nobel Prize–winning economist Milton Friedman, this opening chapter explains how corporations and social expectations of them have evolved over time. This evolution has impacted the purpose and practices of businesses as it relates to their shareholders, stakeholders, and society.

Chapter 2 delves into the blurring of the lines between the private and public sectors in the United States, where traditionally public functions are privatized while at the same time the government is taking a larger role in private enterprises. Drawing from government and business actions during the COVID-19 pandemic and other recent crises, this chapter describes how we became a government incorporated by business principles as well as a marketplace dominated by public policies. In doing so, it explains how this convergence between the public and private sectors has created a new path for social progress in the form of corporate social activism.

Chapter 3 analyzes how the expansion of corporate legal rights and political influence by courts and Congress over the last few decades has catalyzed corporate social activism. Tracing legal and political campaign developments resulting from land-mark Supreme Court decisions, this chapter explores the social impact that recent large waves of money into politics has had on activism and capitalism in American life.

THE NEW BUSINESS OF CHANGE

Moving from systemic origins of corporate social activism to real-world effects, the book next turns the lens and focuses on specific episodes of contemporary corporate social activism to highlight the latest dynamics in the new business of social change. Through a trio of chapters, the middle section of the book examines how contemporary corporate social activism can help effectuate local and national change during an era of parti-san gridlock and political dysfunction.

Chapter 4 examines how local issues become national issues and how national movements become global movements in the context of an awakened society through a powerful blending of activism, capitalism, and technology. Using the case studies of the Ice Bucket Challenge, a North Carolina discriminatory bath-room law, the NFL's Washington Football Team, and the Con-federate flag in South Carolina, this chapter explains how local activists can attract the national attention of businesses and leverage corporate powers and tools to effectuate social change.

Chapter 5 studies how capitalists and activists can serve as a check and backstop on harmful government actions during a time where hyperpartisanship has weakened political checks and balances. This chapter reviews some of the most controversial actions of the Trump administration, like the "Muslim travel ban," Charlottesville, the family separation immigration policies, and the failed insurrection near the end of his term in office. It also highlights the ways in which activists and capitalists can work together to restrain and mitigate some of the worst impulses of government when political checks are lacking.

Chapter 6 spotlights how activists and capitalists can tackle the difficult endemic social issues of race and gender discrimination that have plagued our society, in creative and practical ways that have long evaded meaningful corrective political action. Recalling the events surrounding the #MeToo movement and the killing of George Floyd, this chapter delves into how corporate social activism can lead to innovations in social change through the use of finance, entrepreneurship, technology, and media. It narrates how progress can be made on highly charged and seemingly intractable social issues that our politics seem unwilling or unable to address in a serious manner.

PROMISES AND PERILS

The book closes with a quartet of chapters that considers the promises and perils inherent in corporate social activism and how activists and capitalists could best navigate the road ahead in an urgent present and into a hopeful future. The final chapters highlight the structural benefits and harms for activists, capitalists, and society as corporate social activism gains influence and preference.

Chapter 7 looks at how corporate social activism can create better capitalists and better activists through collaborations to create new means for social progress. Using the works of the

Gates Foundation on global health and JPMorgan Chase in Detroit as case studies, this chapter demonstrates the ways in which activism and capitalism can fuse in a mutually beneficial way toward creating better businesses, better markets, and a better society.

Turning from the light to the shadows, Chapter 8 considers the dark side of corporate social activism, exposing the risks inherent in this new business of social change. It explains how contemporary corporate social activism could polarize an already fragmented marketplace, marginalize important social issues, corrode democratic values, and whitewash corporate misdeeds. It warns of becoming overly reliant on corporate social activism as the only means for social change, to the detriment of diminishing democratic institutions and processes. It reminds us that no matter how successful capitalists and activists are in working together outside of government, there is still no substitute for good, effective democratic government.

Chapter 9 returns to the light and critically imagines how contemporary corporate social activism will continue to grow, mature, and evolve. Using the evolution of the ice cream company Ben & Jerry's as a starting point, it forecasts that corporate social activism will become both more local and more global over time; and it will attract more attention and scrutiny for capitalists and activists working on the frontlines of social change.

Lastly, Chapter 10 sets forth key principles and guideposts for navigating the shifting terrain of business and social change in the coming years and decades while being mindful that there are no clear roadmaps or rules for the road ahead. Drawing lessons from all of the previous chapters, this final chapter recommends workable first principles for capitalists and activists as they move forward together during this revolutionary period in business and activism.

THE HOPEFUL JOURNEY AHEAD

What happened on Valentine's Day 2018 in Parkland, Florida, was a story of tragedy, but what happened in the days that followed was a story of triumph. Ordinary people—young and old, teachers and students, parents and children, Republicans and Democrats—found the activist within, marched, organized, and worked to combat the scourge of gun violence in the United States. And many executives—moved by the activism of their shareholders, consumers, customers, and fellow citizens—leveraged the powers and influence of their business enterprises to aid in this difficult social issue. Together, capitalists and activists were able to make more progress than political leaders have tried and failed to do on their own for years. Together, capitalists and activists offered a different path toward progress during an era of dysfunctional politics.

To be sure, recognizing the virtues and mutual gains that can be had from capitalists and activists working together is not a denial of their faults and foibles. Recognizing the significant good that capitalists can bring about for society does not blind us to the serious harms that they can sometimes create or perpetuate in society. Recognizing the transformative power wielded by activists does not deny the obstacles that they can sometimes present for policymaking. Just as humans are neither all good nor all bad, their institutional and collectively efforts at capitalism and activism are neither all good nor all bad.

We often see activists and capitalists as two different and disconnected groups of people.

In one group are people who toil nobly and selflessly for the public good. In the other group are people who work avariciously and selfishly for private wealth. Two disparate groups chasing different dreams in society, one for social progress and the other for private profit. One of people who march and pro-test for priceless change, the other of people who labor and strive for princely sums.

Yet this bifurcated view is too narrow; it ignores the contra-dictions, complexities, and richness of human beings. A being that the poet renders as large, contradicting, and containing mul-titudes. A being that can work for a giant corporation *and* rally peers to challenge unfair corporate practices. A being that can demonstrate for climate change *and* invest in oil and car compa-nies. A being that can love their high-paying office job *and* take days off to march for a higher minimum wage. A being that can protest for gender equality *and* patronize businesses that perpet-uate systemic sexism. A being that can appreciate the prosperity of profit *and* fight to alleviate poverty.

Finding opportunities for collaboration between capitalists and activists while seeing their inconsistencies is not a denial or discounting of their failings. Rather, it is a recognition of our own inconsistencies and impurities—and our ability to perse-vere and push forward in spite of them.

Capitalist enterprises and activist enterprises are ultimately both human enterprises. They reflect the contradictions, com-plexities, and richness of the human beings that create them, own them, patronize them, move them, work for them, and manage them. They are imperfect and impure, just like the ded-icated flawed people behind them. Too much progress has been needlessly impeded by arbitrary notions of purity and perfec-tion. Such notions have prevented us from seeing capitalists and activists properly—to our detriment.

For too long, we have been seeing capitalists and activists wrong. We have been seeing them disparately, detached and disjointed from one another. Perhaps that limited and impov-erished view was accurate in the past, but it is no longer so. In truth, the social capital that activists possess and seek to turn into lasting policy often intertwines with the economic capital that capitalist possess and seek to turn into sustainable profits. What appears in the pages that follow is the broader, richer, and more complicated view of capitalists and activists, and the power and progress that may be possible when we see them differently. *The Capitalist and the Activist* is about seeing them right—seeing them as part of one, as part of each of us, as part all of us.

CHAPTER 1

Profit, Purpose, and Progress

N 2015, THE WU-TANG CLAN, the greatest hip-hop group ever, sold just one copy of their seventh studio album, *Once Upon a Time in Shaolin*. It was the only copy, and it was sold at an auction for $2 million. It was at the time the highest price ever paid for a piece of music.

The winning bidder was Martin Shkreli, a young New York City pharmaceutical executive. Shkreli made part of his wealth by acquiring the rights to drugs, then raising their prices exponentially. In 2015, his company, Turing Pharmaceuticals, acquired the rights for Daraprim, a drug used for treating parasitic infections. If untreated, such infections could lead to seizures, birth defects, fever, confusion, blindness, and death. Daraprim is so critical to treating parasitic infections that the World Health Organization (WHO) listed it as an "essential medicine." After acquiring the rights to the drug, Shkreli raised the price of Dara-prim from $13.50 to $750 a pill, a price hike of over 5,400 per-cent! The price hike rendered the drug too expensive for many patients who needed it and engendered serious public back-lash. He was dubbed the "pharma bro," "a morally bankrupt sociopath," and "the most hated man in America."[1] Shkreli was called before Congress for a public shaming, yet he remained unashamed of his actions. In an interview with *Forbes* he stated, "'The attempt to public shame is interesting because everything we've done is legal. . . . My investors expect me to maximize prof-its. That's the ugly, dirty truth."[2] He also wished that he had raised prices higher, as it was his "duty" to do so.[3]

Nearly sixty years before Shkreli's shameless Daraprim pric-ing strategy, another young New Yorker had possessed a valu-able pharmaceutical that could prevent the pain and suffering of thousands of people each year. The pharmaceutical, like Dara-prim, is also listed as an essential medicine by the WHO. That New Yorker was Dr. Jonas Salk, and the pharmaceutical in ques-tion was the polio vaccine. After years of research and funding from the Mellon banking fortune, Dr. Salk and his team devel-oped a safe polio vaccine for public use in 1955 to help rid the world of polio. When legendary CBS reporter Edward R. Mur-row asked Salk who owned the patent to his breakthrough vac-cine, he replied, "Well, the people I would say. There is no patent. Could you patent the sun?"[4]

Had Dr. Salk or his benefactors wanted to profit from his efforts, ingenuity, and good fortune, he and they would have become billionaires. It has been estimated that his polio vaccine would have been worth upward of $7 billion.[5] Yet by making his vaccine free and widely available, Dr. Salk saved hundreds of thousands of lives, prevented millions of people from paralysis, and created nearly $200 billion in direct economic benefit in the

United States alone.[6] He went on to live a revered and purposeful life, working on numerous therapies and vaccines—including one for AIDS—until his death in 1995.

In contrast, Martin Shkreli was arrested for securities fraud a few months after his Daraprim pricing scheme and convicted two years later. He was ultimately sentenced to seven years in prison, and federal authorities seized and later auctioned his assets, including Wu-Tang Clan's *Once Upon a Time in Shaolin*.

The stories of Martin Shkreli and Jonas Salk could not be more different. It is almost unfair to compare the two men. Yet they are reflective of deeper impulses in all of us. A desire for profit and personal gain confronting a desire for altruism and societal progress. Their stories are also illustrative of a long-running debate about American business, its primary beneficiaries, its ultimate purpose, and its role in our lives.

SHAREHOLDERS AND STAKEHOLDERS

Who should a corporation and its executives work for? For so many and for so long, this seemed like a straightforward question with a straightforward answer. Corporations should work to maximize profits for their shareholders. Period. To the extent customers, employees, and others in society benefit from corporate actions, those benefits are secondary to the primary service of shareholders. In a seminal case involving Henry Ford and the Ford Motor Company from 1919, a court held in an often-quoted passage:

> A business corporation is organized and carried
> on primarily for the profit of the stockholders. The
> powers of the directors are to be employed for that
> end. The discretion of directors is to be exercised
> in the choice of means to attain that end, and

does not extend to a change in the end itself, to
the reduction of profits, or to the nondistribution
of profits among stockholders in order to devote
them to other purposes.[7]

Despite the apparently simple and long-settled fact of shareholders being the primary beneficiaries of corporate action, the
reality is more complicated and open. The business law scholar
Lynn Stout argued in her book *The Shareholder Value Myth* that
"contrary to what many believe, U.S. corporate law does not
impose any enforceable legal duty on corporate directors or
executives to maximize profits or share price."[8] Stout and others believed that a narrow and exclusive focus on shareholder
value is harmful for shareholders, businesses, and society. Today,
many argue that corporations are responsible to more than just
their shareholders. They must act for the benefit of customers,
employees, communities, and other stakeholders of society.

This debate surrounding the primary beneficiaries of businesses—shareholders or stakeholders—is not new. American
law and society have long wrestled with this fundamental issue
of business. Contemporary understandings of corporate responsibilities and beneficiaries in the United States harken back to a
post–Great Depression debate between leading business and legal
scholars Adolf A. Berle and E. Merrick Dodd in the 1930s. Berle
argued that corporations are primarily responsible to their share-
holder-owners. Dodd, in contrast, argued that corporations are
responsible to their shareholders *and* other constituencies that
may be affected by corporate actions. For Dodd, a corporation
is an "economic institution, which has a social service as well as
a profit-making function."[9] Dodd believed that an unreasonably
narrow focus on shareholder interests alone would stifle corporate
efforts to act for enhancing social welfare beyond pure profit.

This groundbreaking debate about the inherent function of corporations would evolve over time. Following the New Deal and World War II, the debates surrounding the social responsibility of corporations re-emerged as a major issue in the 1950s, 1960s, and 1970s. Leading figures in law, politics, and business supported the view that corporations have obligations to constituencies beyond their shareholders. David Rockefeller, heir to the Rockefeller fortune and chairman of Chase Manhattan Bank (the precursor to today's JPMorgan Chase), opined that "the old concept that the owner of a business had a right to use his property as he pleased to maximize profits, has evolved into the belief that ownership carries certain binding social obligations."[10]

Furthermore, in the wake of the Vietnam War and Watergate, labor unions, social activists, consumer advocates, and others pushed large corporations to do more for the public interest as a rebellion against the old order. As a result of this wave of activism, major corporations like General Motors and Eastman Kodak felt significant pressure to do more than benefit their shareholders and balance sheets. In response, these corporations—whether freely or begrudgingly—made significant contributions to social endeavors and local communities.

PURPOSE AND PROFIT

The evolving debates during this period about the targeted beneficiaries of corporate actions also raised more fundamental questions about business: namely, what should be the chief purpose of a corporation? If corporations exist to serve their shareholders, to what end? If corporations exist to serve multiple stakeholders in society, what is expected of them?

Proponents of a stakeholders-oriented view of business saw corporations as a vehicle for not only long-term sustainable value-enhancing corporations, but also for social progress. To them, the primary corporate purpose should be to enhance the social welfare of shareholders, employees, customers, and other stakeholders in society. In contrast, those who opposed a stakeholders-oriented view of business saw the corporation as merely a contractual and financial vehicle for generating profit in an open marketplace with little or no regard for social values, except those directly related to their business. To them, the primary purpose of a corporation should be to maximize profits for their shareholders.

The most famous proponent of shareholder profit maximization as the primary purpose of corporations was Milton Friedman, the Nobel Prize–winning free market economist. In 1970, he authored one of the most influential pieces of business writing or arguably any writing, in a *New York Times Magazine* article titled "The Social Responsibility of Business Is to Increase Its Profits."[11] Friedman unabashedly stated, "there is one and only one social responsibility of business—to use its resources and engage in activities designed to increase its profits so long as it stays within the rules of the game."[12]

For Friedman and others who shared his view on corporations, using the corporation as a vehicle for social progress and stakeholder interests rather than purely for profit posed profound adverse consequences for democratic society and free markets.[13] Friedman warned that deviations of corporate focus from shareholder profit to a broader social responsibility would "clearly harm the foundations of a free society."[14] For Friedman, shifting corporate focus away from profits and shareholders to social welfare and stakeholders would lead to a breakdown of the free market system and democratic institutions: "the doctrine of 'social responsibility' involves the acceptance of the socialist view that political mechanisms, not market mechanisms, are the appropriate way to determine the allocation of scarce resources to alternative uses."[15]

A year after Friedman's article, Lewis Powell, prior to his Supreme Court appointment, authored an influential memo to the U.S. Chamber of Commerce recommending a comprehensive and aggressive response against a perceived "broad attack" on the American economic system from critics and socialists.[16] Powell called for corporations to engage more actively in shaping scholarship, public discourse, and politics through a sustained influence campaign that would reach campuses, media, and government. His recommendations would be widely adopted by large corporations in the ensuing years to help perpetuate Friedman's free-market view of corporate purpose.

Friedman's corporate perspective came at a particularly fitting historical moment with the ascendency of Ronald Reagan. The resounding election of Reagan in 1980 ushered in an era of smaller government and bigger business. Friedman became an economic advisor to candidate and then president Reagan. Reagan and his free-market acolytes built on Friedman's economic and corporate vision by cutting corporate taxes, reducing business regulation, and giving private market forces more freedom to operate in the United States. A boom of mergers, acquisitions, and leveraged buyout activities glamorized Wall Street bankers and corporate raiders as they zealously worked to boost stock prices and increase private returns during an era of lower taxes and declining regulation.

The Reagan Revolution elevated the profit-driven purpose of corporate America to a sacred creed for many political and business leaders. By the time Reagan left office in 1989, his view of limited government, free markets, and profit-driven corporations became akin to an article of national faith. As Reagan remarked in his farewell address:

> Through more and more rules and regulations and confiscatory taxes, the Government was taking more of our freedom. . . . And I hope we have once again reminded people that man is not free unless government is limited. There's a clear cause and effect here that is as neat and predictable as a law of physics: as government expands, liberty contracts.[17]

At the time of Friedman's passing in 2006, Larry Summers, a leading and influential economic thinker for Democratic presidents of his generation, said of Friedman, "Any honest Democrat will admit that we are now all Friedmanites. Mr. Friedman . . . never held elected office but he has had more influence on economic policy as it is practiced around the world today than any other modern figure."[18]

On the fiftieth anniversary of Friedman's seminal essay, in 2020, the *New York Times* called the essay "a free market manifesto that changed the world."[19]

Despite its enormous influence, the Reagan-Friedman view of business and capitalism was not universally embraced in its own time or in the ensuing decades. The profit-first, profit-only view of business under the Reagan Revolution raised new concerns about the social obligations of corporations beyond shareholders to constituencies like employees, creditors, customers, and local communities. This was motivated in part by the fact that despite significant stock market increases and income growth for the wealthy, many working-class Americans were left behind in the economic growth.

Ultimately, Reagan's "shining city upon a hill" predicated on a corporate purpose of profit-seeking in a free market cast a long shadow on the millions of people left looking up at that hill and wanting something different. During Reagan's tenure, numerous states passed corporate constituency statutes to permit corporations to consider the impact of deals on nonshareholder stakeholders, encouraging companies to think of corporate purpose beyond the cold, narrow confines of profits.[20] This tension of corporate purpose between narrow corporate profit and broader social progress would force law, business, and society to evolve in their views about corporations in the United States.

FROM SOCIALLY RESPONSIBLE TO SOCIALLY ACTIVE

The debates about shareholders versus stakeholders and corporate profit versus social progress were recast into a larger discourse about corporate social responsibility and corporate social activism at the beginning of the twenty-first century following the booms and excesses of the 1980s and 1990s.

The notion that corporations have some social responsibility has become widely accepted, even if there are legitimate disagreements about how businesses could best carry out their social obligations. The interesting questions today are not about *whether* corporate social responsibility should exist, but about *how* it should exist. Today, almost all prominent corporations, from long-established ones like Apple, Disney, and Nike to upstarts like Airbnb, Lyft, and Twitter have formal corporate social responsibility programs. They issue formal reports touting their socially beneficial efforts in a range of areas, and their websites actively update the public on their responsible actions as good corporate citizens. For example, Apple, one of the world's most valuable and most respected companies, publishes reports concerning the company's efforts on environmental impact, supplier responsibility, and diversity and inclusion. Business software giant Salesforce even includes social responsibility disclosures in its annual report on Form 10-K, which traditionally contains primarily business and financial information. The Fortune Global 500 companies alone have spent billions of dollars annually in their social responsibility efforts in recent years.[21]

Yet over time, being merely socially responsible became insufficient for the demands and expectations of a changing marketplace and society. Corporate social responsibility alone seemed too passive, too insular, and too self-serving. In a world that seemed to be literally on fire from climate change and social unrest, corporate social responsibility appeared to many as a privileged exercise in self-improvement, however sincere or not. Corporate self-improvement was not enough for many engaged consumers and citizens; active corporate social improvement through activism was desired and called for.

Many in society and within corporations have come to expect businesses and executives, particularly those at large public companies, to engage with the critical social issues of the day. Increasingly, businesses are expected by their shareholders, communities, consumers, employees, and executives to engage in social activism on issues directly or indirectly related to their core operations. Contentious social issues like racial justice, income inequality, gun violence, immigration reform, gender equality, and climate change have all become part of many corporate agendas. Silence and indifference are becoming less the norm. The days of simply ignoring social issues or writing a check are gone. Corporations are now frequently expected to engage in social issues through public statements, sponsorships, partnerships, and policies supporting a position or a cause. Being a socially responsible corporation now also means being a socially active corporation.

This evolution from corporate social responsibility to corporate social activism should be of little surprise, given how corporations have so vociferously promoted themselves as good, responsible citizens of society. If corporations had consistently presented themselves as largely amoral profit-generating machines, engaging them or expecting them to engage in social activism would likely have been less understandable and less appealing. But because businesses have long promoted themselves to their shareholders and the world as moral and socially conscious entities engaged in the community, it is logical to expect that they engage in social activism. Not surprisingly, interested parties and activists for social issues have sought to use the powers and platforms of businesses to help them achieve their goals. Similarly, society and the marketplace have come to expect corporations to actively engage in the important social issues of the day like never before.

A NEW CORPORATE SOCIAL ACTIVISM

Corporate social activism itself is not entirely new, but the times, tools, and context of the present have made contemporary corporate social activism meaningfully different in kind, not just degree.

Corporations have played a critical role in social activism throughout U.S. history. Because businesses, their executives, and their consumers do not exist in a social vacuum, corporations have taken on different roles in the ebbs and flows of social change. Sometimes they were on the right side of history; other times they were not. Episodes from the civil rights movement of the 1960s highlight the various corporate roles in social activism on the defining social issue of that period.

During that period, corporations served as the settings for many acts of social activism and civil disobedience. Sit-ins and boycotts of corporations that refused to serve African Americans on an equal basis were common. Notably, in 1960, four African American students—Joseph McNeil, Franklin McCain, Ezell Blair, Jr., and David Richmond—led a sit-in at a segregated Woolworth department store lunch counter in Greensboro, North Carolina, that inspired sit-ins and boycotts throughout the South, ultimately leading to the desegregation of many stores.[22] The Greensboro case and the iconic images involving Woolworth poignantly illustrate the important role corporations can have in the fight for social change, serving as both places and participants that hinder or help to facilitate progress.

In the 1960s, many corporations openly took positions supporting civil rights even in the face of serious and dangerous resistance. Many businesses played a crucial role in lobbying Presidents John Kennedy and Lyndon Johnson in the epic political battles that ultimately led to the passage and enforcement of the landmark Civil Rights Act of 1964 and Civil Rights Act of 1968.[23] Some businesses gave financial and other support to civil rights leaders and civil rights organizations like the National Urban League and the National Association for the Advancement of Colored People (NAACP).[24] For instance, Coca-Cola rallied white business and political leaders in Atlanta to celebrate Dr. Martin Luther King, Jr., in the face of racist opposition, after he was awarded the Nobel Peace Prize in 1964.[25]

Many businesses also desegregated on their own in defiance of historical custom, welcoming African American employees and customers before it was widely accepted. Businesses in Charlotte and Dallas desegregated their facilities even as many government buildings and public facilities remained segregated in those cities. Major corporations like Avon, Xerox, and McDonald's also led the way in integrating African Americans into their hiring practices, marketing plans, and investment initiatives.[26] Smaller Black-owned businesses and their executives also played a significant role alongside social activists during this period.

While there were many companies on the right side of history, many businesses were also on the wrong side. After the passage of the Civil Rights Act of 1964, it became unlawful to discriminate on the basis of race in public places. Unfortunately, many businesses in the South publicly rejected and flouted the newly enacted federal law.

Notably, the Heart of Atlanta Motel brazenly defied the law by refusing to rent rooms to Black customers. The hotel's owner sued the federal government, challenging the validity of the Civil Rights Act of 1964 to govern a private business on the basis of interstate commerce. With a unanimous decision in *Heart of Atlanta Motel, Inc. v. United States*, the Supreme Court held that Congress had the power to ban racial discrimination under the Constitution: "The action of the Congress in the adoption of the Act as applied here to a motel which concededly serves interstate travelers is within the power granted it by the Commerce Clause."[27]

This landmark decision expanded congressional powers to combat racial discrimination. As a response, some political and business interests pushed back and worked to repeal or curb the effects of the Civil Rights Acts of 1964 and 1968 through discriminatory practices like redlining in housing against African Americans. Historian Richard Rothstein, in his remarkable book *The Color of Law: A Forgotten History of How Our Government Segregated America*, chronicled the systemic discriminatory practices and policies of housing discrimination against African Americans and their longstanding and wide-ranging impacts that reverberate to this day.[28]

The aforementioned varying roles that corporations played in social activism during the civil rights movement of the 1960s are not unique to that movement. Corporations have played a significant role—positive and negative—in almost every major social movement in the United States after World War II. At times, some businesses helped to entrench the status quo—notably during the Jim Crow era. At other times, some businesses were on the vanguard of change—integrating or voluntarily offering benefits to certain employees in advance of legal mandates requiring them to do so. Computing giant IBM, for instance, offered benefits to its gay employees years before the federal or local laws required businesses to do so in IBM's many business locations.

The varying roles of businesses throughout historical episodes of activism should not be surprising. Businesses understandably and inevitably reflect and react to the views of their constituencies—their executives, employees, customers, and shareholders—who were also of competing views on this or that issue. As such, corporate social activism, like activism itself, is not entirely new.

Contemporary corporate social activism, however, is different because it takes place during a singular historical moment, in which business and government are converging, and corporate political power is ascending in the context of an awakened society equipped with unprecedented tools and technology to communicate, capitalize, and organize. Contemporary corporate social activism gives ordinary citizens, consumers, and shareholders unprecedented power and influence to leverage corporate resources to help effectuate social progress. Business executives today have to worry not only about shareholder activists agitating for corporate reforms, but also about social activists agitating for social reforms.

In response to these changing tides, in 2019, the Business Roundtable, an association of leading CEOs of the country's biggest companies, put forth a remarkable statement defining corporate purpose as a "fundamental commitment to *all* our stakeholders."[29] This includes customers, employees, suppliers, communities, and shareholders. Whether this statement translates into genuine, sustained action from all the signatories remains to be seen, but it is clear that CEOs see and hear the changes happening around them.

Since the establishment of the Dutch East India Company in the year 1602, and perhaps even earlier, corporations have been reinventing themselves and their purposes in accordance with their worlds, and their times. All corporations are capable of being born again. Some just do not know that they are dying or dead. The advent of this new corporate social activism represents the next reincarnation in business and society.

CHAPTER 2

Government Incorporated

JAY CARNEY WENT FROM WORKING for one of the most powerful men in the world . . . to working for one of the most powerful men in the world.

Carney's path to these heights was not a straight or swift one, though there were some hallmarks common to those who near the apex of power. He attended an elite prep school before Yale University. Following Yale, he worked as a local reporter in Miami before going to *Time* magazine. At *Time*, he served as a foreign correspondent in Moscow during the twilight of the Cold War, then covered the White House, and ultimately became *Time*'s DC bureau chief.

On November 4, 2008, Barack Obama was elected as the forty-fourth president of the United States. About a month after the election, Carney resigned his senior post at *Time* and joined the administration as communications director for Vice President-elect Joe Biden. Three years later, in 2011, Carney became the Obama White House press secretary, helping to shape the president's message, vision, and policies at home and abroad. He served in this role for more than three years, one of the longest tenures in recent administrations, before resigning in 2014.

After leaving the White House, Carney assumed the position of senior vice president for global corporate affairs at Amazon, one of the most valuable and important companies in the world. He reported directly to Jeff Bezos, Amazon founder and one of the world's wealthiest people. Carney's position as one of Amazon's most senior executives put him in charge of helping to shape Amazon's public affairs with governments and consumers around the world.

Jay Carney's journey from the White House to the C-suites of Amazon is both remarkable—and relatively common. As the business world draws on talented and well-connected individuals from government after their public service, his trajectory is a well-traveled path. This is true not only for lower-level White House and congressional staffers but also for public servants near the highest levels of power. As a prominent example, Dick Cheney became the chairman and CEO of Halliburton, a Fortune 500 energy company, after serving as secretary of defense in the first Bush administration. Vice President Dan Quayle became the chairman of Cerberus Global Investments, a multi-billion-dollar private equity firm with operations around the world.

Conversely, government drawing from the private sector leadership and talent pool is nothing new either. Franklin Delano Roosevelt chose Joseph Kennedy, a financier and patriarch of the Kennedy family, to serve as the first chairman of the U.S. Securities and Exchange Commission. Joseph Kennedy's son

John Fitzgerald Kennedy became president and drew widely from the business world for his administration. He chose Robert McNamara, the young president of the Ford Motor Company, to serve as his secretary of defense. More recently, Dick Cheney returned from Halliburton to public life as vice president of the United States in the second Bush administration, which also enlisted other business leaders to serve their country. For instance, Hank Paulson, the chairman and CEO of Goldman Sachs, was brought in to serve as the Treasury secretary.

This longstanding bipartisan revolving door between government and business reflects the inconvenient realities of life in a capitalistic democratic republic. On the one hand, when working well, this revolving door allows businesses and government to draw on talented, ethical individuals from the private and public sectors to serve the interests of both shareholders and citizens. On the other hand, this revolving door can lead to corrosive cronyism and corruption that eats away at the integrity of both business and government as narrow interests are served, to the detriment of shareholders and citizens.

Beyond exposing the tensions in the uneasy relationship between business and government, the revolving door pathology also reflects and reveals large truths about the boundaries of business and government, about the divisions of private and public in the United States today. It seems that there is perhaps less of a revolving door and more of a skybridge connecting the powers of business and government into one blended superstructure. It appears that the old boundaries of public and private are less clear and less meaningful than before; what was once thought to be public is becoming more private, and vice versa. Ideas and concepts of the private markets become part of public discourse, and ideas and concepts of public governance become part of private business discussions. This emerging convergence of business and government, of private and public, has had profound implications for change and progress in business and society.

PUBLIC BECOMING PRIVATE

The public sphere is becoming more private. Businesses are exerting their influence on traditional, public government functions like never before. In many cases they have taken over, in part or in whole, functions that previously were purely public. In describing this large ongoing trend of privatization of the public sphere, David Rothkopf, author and former undersecretary of commerce in the Clinton administration, observed, "Corporations have grown in influence worldwide and in every instance have played a role in paring away key prerogatives of the state."[1]

Today, private for-profit universities are common, as are private prisons, law enforcement, tax collection, and military forces. The corporate encroachment into traditional governmental functions even extends into areas of foreign affairs, foreign aid, and national defense. As revealed by the scholar Allison Stanger in her book *One Nation Under Contract: The Outsourcing of American Power and the Future of Foreign Policy*, government functions of diplomacy, development, and defense have actually grown more and more reliant on private contractors over the years.[2] In recent years, over 80 percent of the budgets of the State and Defense departments have gone to grants and contracts for private businesses, often to perform tasks that were previously done by public servants.[3]

Large corporations today operate like "private empires," to borrow the term the author and journalist Steve Coll used to describe Exxon Mobil in its heyday in the early 2000s.[4] During that period Exxon had more than 2.5 million shareholders, operations in almost every country, and annual sales of around four hundred billion dollars, which rivals the gross domestic product of Sweden.[5] BlackRock, the world's largest asset manager, oversees a multi-trillion-dollar portfolio that rivals the total currency reserves of China and Japan combined.[6] Walmart employs more than two million individuals and "supports an employee/family community of eight to ten million, which is about the size of Austria, Switzerland, or Israel, and larger than a hundred other countries."[7] In fact, besides the government, Walmart is the largest employer in over twenty states in recent years.[8]

Furthermore, today's trillion-dollar tech giants like Apple, Amazon, Alphabet (Google), and Microsoft are each worth more than the gross domestic products (GDPs) of countries like Saudi Arabia, Switzerland, Belgium, and Thailand. If the market caps of these tech giants were ranked as national GDP, they would each be ranked among the twenty-five most valuable countries in the world.

The rise of omnipresent technology companies is one of the most visible aspects of the rise of private companies in the traditional arena of government. This was made clear in the initial months of the COVID-19 pandemic, when people grew heavily reliant on these large technology companies for essential goods, services, and information. Today, Facebook and other major technology companies like Amazon and Google oversee communities that number in the billions, rendering them nation-like in their population, power, and influence. Facebook has over 2.7 billion monthly active users in its namesake platform.[9] That figure rises to over 3 billion active users if one includes its other platforms, like WhatsApp, Instagram, and Messenger.[10] If Facebook was a country, it would be the largest in the world by population if one used its active monthly users as a proxy for headcount. It generates over $70 billion in annual revenues, which would easily place it in the top one hundred countries in the world as measured by GDP.[11] Facebook also has an independent oversight board that acts like a supreme court to adjudicate disputes with its members, and it is developing its own digital currency. Perhaps we should not be surprised that one of Facebook's most senior executives is Nick Clegg, a former deputy prime minister of the United Kingdom, someone well versed in running an actual sovereign state.

'This trend of the public becoming private—of public goods and services becoming private goods and services—is so pronounced that the president of the United States is often considered the CEO of the country. The election of Donald Trump in 2016 in some ways was a watershed moment of this merger of public and private, this corporatization of government, as a self-professed corporate CEO became the leader of the country and the free world.

PRIVATE BECOMING PUBLIC

Just as the public sphere is becoming more private, the private sphere is also becoming more public. As businesses have moved into the traditional province of government, the government has similarly encroached into the traditional space of private enterprise. This movement by the government is precipitated in part by recent crises that expose the shortcomings and failings of private market mechanisms.

During the great financial crisis of 2008 and 2009, the federal government acquired controlling interests in some of the country's largest and most influential corporations, like AIG, Citigroup, and General Motors, as a way to bail out these businesses to prevent them from failing.[12] It has been estimated that the federal government expended over $7 trillion in bailout funds during this period.[13] At one point during the crisis, the federal government became the largest and most influential shareholder for the largest insurance company, the largest banks, and the largest automaker in the country. In addition to taking large direct ownership stakes in some of the largest companies in the country, the government exercised more oversight as well as management powers over these businesses. For instance, in 2009, exercising its prerogative as majority shareholder, the government fired the CEO of General Motors, Rick Wagoner.[14]

More recently, during the coronavirus pandemic, state governments and the federal government took significant steps that directly affected private businesses for the sake of public health. States shut down all nonessential businesses during the initial surge of the pandemic in 2020. Numerous states mandated the wearing of masks inside stores. Restaurants and bars were ordered to close at first, then permitted to have only outdoor dining or limited indoor dining in many states.

In response to the pandemic, the federal government took unprecedented action in connection with private businesses. The federal government ordered companies to produce personal protective equipment and other medical supplies.[15] Furthermore, the federal government and the Federal Reserve took unprecedented actions by providing trillions of dollars in direct economic relief to individuals and businesses.[16] Congress passed legislation that gave forgivable loans to small businesses in exchange for those businesses' assurance that they would not lay off employees. The Federal Reserve purchased billions of dollars in securities of companies in the capital markets to ensure that businesses had adequate capital during this period of great distress. And in the summer of 2021, the federal government mandated the vaccination or testing of millions of private company employees around the country.

Today, for many businesses—small and large—the government is their most important business partner, especially during times of crisis. Public intervention into private businesses during crises blurs and changes the traditional boundaries between the private spheres of business and the public sphere of government. These public actions during crisis alter norms and social expectations about government intervention in business. Over time, government policymakers have become more emboldened to directly enter into the private sphere of business beyond traditional regulation, to directly engage individual businesses on operational matters like customer service, pricing, and advertising. Similarly, businesses have become more mindful and accepting of the specter of government involvement in their boardrooms and executive suites.

TWO CONVERGING PATHS TO PROGRESS

President Abraham Lincoln stated, "The legitimate object of government is to do for a community of people whatever they need to have done, but cannot do at all, or cannot so well do, for themselves in their separate and individual capacities."[17] Conventionally, it was expected that businesses should focus on profit generation using private market mechanisms, while government should focus on public concerns that cannot readily be addressed by the marketplace. Put simply, government takes care of so-called public goods and services like national defense and law enforcement, and businesses take care of most private goods and services.

Yet in contemporary American society, the public responsibilities of government and the private endeavors of business have blurred and blended as government and business frequently act and influence one another in interchangeable ways. As former dean of Harvard Law School Martha Minow observed in her book *Partners Not Rivals: Privatization and the Public Good*, "So many activities cross the conventional [public-private] boundaries that the boundaries themselves start to shift and blur."[18] In today's society the distinct historical pathways of public institutions and private enterprises, with their divergent but complementary objectives, have converged.

This convergence of government and business has changed much about the business of government, the governing of businesses, and the activism that occurs where they intersect. This convergence is a key factor contributing to the rise of contemporary corporate social activism, in addition to an evolving understanding of corporate purpose and responsibility, as discussed in the previous chapter.

Given this public-private convergence, activists seeking social change will do so not only through the traditional public channels of government and politics but also through the newer private channels of business and commerce. Why simply continue to seek progress only through politics, lobbying, and other traditional forms of public sector advocacy and activism when there is an additional path? Why not seek progress through and with corporations and the private sector as well?

When confronted with these questions, more and more activists choose to pursue change and progress via the converging paths of government and business. The old way of conceptualizing either public or private avenues for change has been rendered a false choice. On issue after issue the preferred choice is one that engages both public policymakers and institutions as well as private businesses and executives.

This preferred public-private path often uses private commerce to make progress on social issues by fusing capitalism and activism to engage with the public political process. Activists will often leverage the resources of businesses to amplify their voices to the public and to policymakers who might be more accessible and receptive to voices that come with the imprimaturs of business.

Today, one can effectuate change and progress on important social issues like voting rights, racial justice, income inequality, gun violence, immigration reform, gender equality, and climate change by changing laws and public policies *and* by changing the institutional practices and priorities at major corporations. For instance, climate change activists could choose to only work through Congress and executive branch agencies to get new legislation or regulation to help their cause, and they could also choose to work through and with big businesses on their energy practices. In recent years, many climate activists have found more success working with large companies like Apple, Amazon, and Walmart and even oil companies like Shell and British Petroleum than with the federal government on new commitments and investments to curb their carbon footprints.

Moreover, contemporary political dysfunction and obstructionist partisanship have made these new corporate channels of social change and progress that much more appealing relative to the traditional public channels of government. Efforts toward change and progress too often find their death and purgatory in the crucible of a congressional committee, a threatened filibuster, or an endless executive branch–sanctioned rulemaking process, despite strong popular support. Even sensible ideas and proposals can go nowhere when the worst impulses of partisan politics poison any chance for progress. Nowadays few ordinary citizens look to Washington, DC, as the place for swift, smart, and sensible solutions.

Notably, during the coronavirus pandemic, public health advocates inside and outside of government struggled to convince many states and municipalities to mandate mask wearing and social distancing indoors because of politics. This happened during a pandemic that was killing thousands of people a day, with every reputable scientist advocating for these public health safeguards. Nevertheless, despite the lack of political will for something so practical, many big retailers with outlets around the country, like Target, Walmart, and CVS, all mandated masks in their stores nationwide for their tens of millions of customers to help curb the spread of the virus, even in states and cities where governors and mayors refused to issue sensible mandates and guidance to protect their citizens. Similarly, many big businesses took the lead in encouraging and mandating vaccination of their employees for the sake of public health when many national and local politicians refused to do so.

Given the all-too-common political dysfunction and gridlock in government these days, change and progress on tough social issues via corporate social activism not only is more appealing but also can be more effective. Corporations and their executives can move more swiftly than government to accommodate change, customer sentiments, and social norms in ways that a dysfunctional political process simply cannot.

To be clear, the appeal and effectiveness of corporate social activism on some issues does not mean that private for-profit enterprises should serve as substitutes for public democratic institutions. Corporate social activism is not a market-based alternative to government, nor should it be. There is simply no substitute for good, effective government in a democracy. Rather, social change and progress through business could and should serve as a complement to the efforts of government and the political process. However, as our politics and national government have grown so dysfunctional, people have turned to businesses and business leaders to help tackle the challenges that confront American society while still trying to fix our political processes.

The choice for social activists is no longer an *either/or* proposition, but is now a *both/and* proposition; they can work through both public and private channels of government and business to effectuate social change, legal reform, and new policies in contemporary society. This *both/and* proposition manifests in a new form of corporate social activism whereby activists and capitalists join forces to address some of society's toughest challenges.

CHAPTER 3

Corporate Rights, Money, and Activism

ANN NIXON WAS BORN ON JANUARY 9, 1902, in Bedford County, Tennessee, a small town outside Nashville.[1] She was the daughter of tenant farmers in the South and the granddaughter of grandparents who recalled Lincoln's Emancipation Proclamation. Her childhood as a Black girl in the South was stained and shackled by the inhumane racism that endured in the generations after the Civil War.

Despite the limitations of segregated life, Ann grew up with a sunny outlook and found love with A. B. Cooper, a dentist. They married, moved to Atlanta, Georgia, and started a family that grew with the arrivals of four children. In Atlanta, she lived a socially and politically active life. She helped start the first Boy Scout troop and a Girls Club for African American youngsters. She befriended Dr. Martin Luther King and worked as a tutor at Ebenezer Baptist Church. Ann registered to vote on Monday, September 1, 1941, but because of the social obstacles imposed on Blacks and women, especially Black women during her time, she did not vote for many years.[2]

In 1981, Ann turned seventy-nine. That same year, hundreds of miles north of Atlanta in New York City, Michael Bloomberg was fired from the investment bank Salomon Brothers. No need to feel sorry for young Michael; the bank gave him $10 million in severance. Bloomberg used that severance to start a company that ultimately bore his name, Bloomberg L.P. The company gained prominence by creating a specialized computer terminal for traders and bankers that delivered real-time financial information and allowed them to communicate and execute trades. This was decades before the creation of the modern internet. The Bloomberg terminal has become one of the most indispensable and valuable technologies on Wall Street. A Bloomberg terminal costs over $20,000 to lease annually, and over 320,000 terminals are leased each year for an astounding $6.4 billion in annual revenue.[3] Due in large part to that namesake terminal, Michael Bloomberg became one of the world's richest people.

In 2001, Bloomberg decided to run for mayor of New York City. A lifelong businessman and Democrat with no political experience, Bloomberg decided to run as a Republican in the largest and most Democratic city in the United States. The dynamics of the campaign were altered by the events of September 11, 2001. Bloomberg was endorsed by the outgoing mayor, Rudy Giuliani, who was riding high after his leadership during the terrorist attack, and Bloomberg won the race. Four years later, Bloomberg was re-elected to a second term.

The fall of 2008 was significant in the life of Michael Bloomberg and Ann Nixon Cooper, and in the life of the United States, for that matter. The country was experiencing the deepest recession since the Great Depression, brought on by an unprecedented financial and economic crisis. Bloomberg's second term as mayor would be coming to an end in about a year, as he was limited to two terms. At the same time, two honorable men from different generations—Senators Barack Obama and John McCain—competed to become the forty-fourth president of the United States.

Rather than accept the eight-year term limit to his tenure as New York City mayor, Bloomberg opened his wallet and lobbied to change the term limit rules so he could serve a third term to help the city through the financial crisis afflicting the country. On October 23, 2008, the New York City Council changed the rules to permit Bloomberg to run for a third term.

About eleven days later, Senator Barack Obama was elected the forty-fourth president of the United States, becoming the first African American to hold the highest office of the land. In his victory speech in Grant Park, Chicago, that night, President-elect Obama cited one person by name—Ann Nixon Cooper. Cooper, then 106, had waited in line earlier that morning in Atlanta to cast her vote for the man who would become the first Black U.S. president. Obama used the century-plus years of Cooper's life as a lens to reflect on "the heartache and the hope; the struggle and the progress" of the country, and what was still possible.[4]

A year later, in 2009, Ann Nixon Cooper passed away and Michael Bloomberg won a third term as New York City mayor. Bloomberg spent a record-breaking $102 million on his campaign.[5] This figure obliterated his previous records of $74 million in his 2001 campaign and $85 million in his 2005 campaign.[6] According to the *New York Times*, Bloomberg spent an astounding $174 per vote to win his third term as mayor![7]

Too often, election winners and their supporters romanticize American politics, believing that their victory was solely the result of extraordinary, yet ordinary individuals like Ann Nixon Cooper coming out in massive numbers in support of their vision and ideas to move the large gears of a democratic republic forward. While there is truth in that romantic narrative, it is an incomplete story. American politics is more and more about money—the people who have it, the politicians who search for it, and the ends that they seek in one another.

American politics is becoming more about billionaires like Michael Bloomberg than about ordinary people. Be it Michael Bloomberg and Tom Steyer on the left, or the Ricketts family and the Kochs on the right, money, moneyed institutions, and moneymen (they are generally men) have become an undeniable force to be reckoned with in American democracy. Landing key billionaires as early financial supporters is arguably one of the most important tasks of any candidate seeking a credible run for high office. While new fundraising platforms like ActBlue have made it easier for politicians to raise funds from small donors online, large donors with corporate ties still play an outsized role in shaping and shifting the political and policymaking machinery.

In the 2020 presidential election cycle, over $14 billion was raised and spent by candidates seeking the presidency.[8] This was a record figure that more than doubled the records established in the 2016 election cycle. Michael Bloomberg alone spent over $1.2 billion in the 2020 cycle with his short-lived $1 billion Democratic primary run, which won him only four delegates from American Samoa.[9]

This influx of money and corporate influence into politics is not an accident of history. As legal scholar and historian Adam Winkler chronicled in his insightful book, *We the Corporations: How American Businesses Won Their Civil Rights*, this influx was the result of a deliberate effort by many to expand corporate political rights through decades of legislation, litigation, and lobbying.[10] Like the convergence of government and business, and the evolution of corporate purpose and responsibility, this expansion of corporate political rights has played a significant role in fostering a new kind of corporate social activism.

CORPORATIONS ARE PEOPLE, MY FRIEND

In 2011 at the Iowa State Fair, during his presidential run against President Obama, Republican nominee Mitt Romney got into a spirited exchange with voters about his tax policies. Some of the voters at the fair wanted him to raise taxes on the wealthy and businesses after Romney had pledged to not raise taxes at all. In defense of his position, Romney uttered a line that affirmed the worst perceptions of him as a wealthy, out-of-touch, lay-off-loving private equity executive: "Corporations are people, my friend."[11]

On its face, Romney's statement seems absurd. People are flesh-and-blood human beings with feelings, memories, and dreams. Our grandparents, our parents, our partners, and our friends are people. Corporations like Walmart, Target, Amazon, Goldman Sachs, and Google are not people. Any young child can tell a person from a nonperson. Yet Romney was not entirely wrong. In the eyes of American law, corporations are viewed as legal persons in much the same way as natural persons like our grandparents, parents, partners, and friends.

The understanding of a corporation as a legal person with certain rights of natural persons is a longstanding hallmark of American law. Chief Justice Marshall famously character-ized the corporation as "an artificial being, invisible, intangi-ble, and existing only in contemplation of law" in the landmark 1819 case *Trustees of Dartmouth College v. Woodward*, where the court established the sanctity of a private corporate charter as a contract between legal persons that is protected under the Constitution.[12]

Since then, the U.S. Supreme Court has constructed an expanding legal patchwork of corporate personhood and corporate rights. The Court has recognized corporations as distinct legal persons that possess contract and property rights for more than two centuries.[13] Over time, the Court has also recognized that corporations possess certain Fourth Amendment rights against searches and seizures and certain First Amendment rights, but no Fifth Amendment protections against self-incrimination or personal privacy protections.[14] More recently, in two landmark cases—*Citizens United* and *Hobby Lobby*—the Court held that corporations possess free speech protections for political contributions and religious liberties. These two relatively recent, seminal cases have had important consequences in the development of contemporary corporate social activism.

CITIZENS UNITED

In the 2010 *Citizens United* case, a conservative nonprofit political organization challenged the Bipartisan Campaign Reform Act. This federal law prohibited corporations and other associations from using general corporate funds to make political expenditures in connection with electioneering communications during restricted periods of a federal election cycle. Citizens United wanted to broadcast a disparaging film about Hillary Clinton during the 2008 election cycle and had received funds for its efforts through a few corporate entities. To be sure, this movie was intended to serve as a full-length negative attack ad against Hillary Clinton. In a 5 to 4 opinion, the Supreme Court held that the campaign finance restriction was unconstitutional when it imposed limitations on the political expenditures of corporations. The opinion declared: "The Court has thus rejected the argument that political speech of corporations or other associations should be treated differently under the First Amendment simply because such associations are not 'natural persons.'"[15]

The *Citizens United* decision profoundly changed American politics. The Court's ruling effectively lifted any limitations on American corporations' political expenditures. The ruling permitted for-profit corporations to use corporate funds for campaign contributions to support candidates and issues. It also permitted wealthy and well-connected individuals to form corporations as vehicles to solicit, collect, and disperse funds, with little to no transparency.

Following the decision, corporate interests expanded upon their previously outsized influence in the political system by injecting even more money into the political process, both directly to campaigns and indirectly through intermediaries like political action committees (PACs), super PACs, and other tax-exempt LLCs, without being subject to stringent disclosure rules about their expenditures and sources of funding. In the 2012 presidential election cycle, the first after *Citizens United*, the *New York Times* reported in a front-page story that as a result of the ruling, businesses now seemed to prefer to "influence campaigns by donating money to tax-exempt organizations that can spend millions of dollars without being subject to the disclosure requirements that apply to candidates."[16] These organizations—often bearing innocuous-sounding names like Preserve America, American Bridge, The Lincoln Project, and For Our Future—have raised hundreds of millions of dollars each election cycle from special interests and business interests to influence elections through ads and other efforts.

Figures from the nonpartisan Center for Responsive Politics highlight the incredible growth of outside spending across the political spectrum following *Citizens United* in each election cycle after the decision. In the 2008 election cycle, outside spending by parties other than the candidates totaled around $574 million.[17] In the 2012 election cycle, outside spending spiked to nearly $1.3 billion.[18] In the 2016 election cycle, outside spending was around $1.7 billion[19] and super PACs raised nearly $1.8 billion.[20] Most recently, in the 2020 election cycle, super PACs raised over $3.1 billion.[21]

This growth in outside spending following *Citizens United* happened on a bipartisan basis. Conservative and liberal outside groups ramped up their fundraising and spending, with business executives playing a leading role to drown out the voices of ordinary Americans. Only about 1 percent of Americans contributed at least $200 in the 2020 election cycle, and only 0.160 percent gave the $2,700 maximum individual limit.[22] According to a *New York Times* report, in recent election cycles, 158 families contributed nearly half of all the money used in presidential campaigns.[23] A 2021 study found that since *Citizens United*, just twelve individuals accounted for "$1 out of every $13 dollars spent in federal elections" from January 2009 to December 2020.[24]

The truth of the matter is that influence inequality makes income inequality look impoverished.

By expanding the free speech rights of corporations in *Citizens United*, the Supreme Court changed politics and policy-making in the United States forever. Politicians now spend an extraordinary amount of time raising money. Political parties in recent years have recommended that their members spend at least four hours a day doing fundraising calls.[25] Four hours a day, every month, every year—even in nonelection years. Furthermore, policy priorities are now shaped more than ever by the moneyed interest groups and wealthy individuals that contribute funds to campaign and party coffers. The voices of ordinary individuals are often distorted, drowned out, and muted by the roaring waves of money in the political process.

Free speech has never cost so much.

HOBBY LOBBY

Four years after *Citizens United*, in 2014, the Supreme Court further expanded corporate political rights in *Burwell v. Hobby Lobby*. In *Hobby Lobby*, shareholders of three family-owned corporations challenged a provision of the Patient Protection and Affordable Care Act of 2010 that required the companies to provide health insurance, including coverage of contraceptive methods for women. Shareholders of the three businesses claimed that compliance with the provisions would force them to "seriously violate" their deeply held Christian beliefs.[26] The Department of Health and Human Services had provided an exemption for religious employers like churches, but the exemption did not extend to for-profit businesses. The businesses claimed that the provision and related exemption violated the Religious Freedom Restoration Act (RFRA), which states that "government shall not substantially burden a person's exercise of religion even if the burden results from a rule of general applicability."[27]

In a 5 to 4 decision, the Court held that for-profit, closely held corporations were persons that could exercise religion, and thus were protected under the RFRA. It opined that for-profit corporations may have concerns beyond profit:

> While it is certainly true that a central objective
> of for-profit corporations is to make money,
> modern corporate law does not require for-profit
> corporations to pursue profit at the expense of
> everything else, and many do not do so. For-profit

corporations, with ownership approval, support
a wide variety of charitable causes, and it is not at
all uncommon for such corporations to further
humanitarian and other altruistic objectives.[28]

Simply put, the Court believed that corporations can exist to
make money, but, like ordinary people, they have other pursuits
beyond income, and it is up to them to prioritize their competing pursuits.

Again, like in *Citizens United*, the Court expanded the legal
understandings of corporate rights relating to pursuing political,
social, and religious aims while giving great deference to corporations to regulate their own affairs in these areas. With its
holdings in *Citizens United* and *Hobby Lobby*, the Court effectively gave businesses the permission to use corporate funds and
resources to engage in political advocacy and social activism
unrelated to their primary commercial pursuits.

FROM MORE CORPORATE RIGHTS
TOWARD MORE CORPORATE ACTIVISM

Given the expansion of corporate rights and powers, especially
after *Citizens United* and *Hobby Lobby*, advocates for social issues
have increasingly sought to use the resources and influence of
businesses to their advantage. Because the law has given corporations such great freedom and deference to engage in issues of
social, political, and religious significance, it is only natural that
activists for such issues try to leverage corporate resources for
their interests.

Similarly, capitalists seeking to effectuate social change would
understandably use their own business platforms to aid them in
achieving their social ends. Corporate executives with strong

personal interests in social causes that they believe align well with the best interests of their companies would be remiss to not reach for the many powerful corporate tools at their disposal. Unsurprisingly, we are witnessing an unprecedented era of activist CEOs that use their companies as platforms to amplify social causes. Business luminaries like Tim Cook of Apple, Marc Benioff of Salesforce, Jeff Bezos of Amazon, and Jamie Dimon of JPMorgan Chase have all taken very public stances on social issues like LGBTQ rights, homelessness, education access, and racial inequality.

Whether this rise in corporate social activism is right and good is subject to legitimate debate and discussion, but what is not debatable is its existence and ascendency. In many ways, its ascendency is understandable. If you cared deeply about an issue or cause, wouldn't you try to get the most powerful people in the world to help you in your efforts, in your cause? Because of legal expansions in corporate rights and changes in corporate social practice, the most powerful people in the world in many contexts are corporations and the people who run them. Corporations are like superheroes (or supervillains) in many ways. They possess a (liability) shield, never die, leverage the powers of others as their own, and move the world through their actions. As such, when activists need aid to help them in their causes to tackle the challenges confronting society, they turn to corporations. This once unexpected alliance between capitalists and activists is now the driving force behind so many social causes.

CHAPTER 4

Everything Is Your Business

VERYONE WAS DOING IT. And everyone was publicly challenged to do it. Celebrities. Public officials. High schoolers. College students. Business leaders. Parents. Grandparents. The queen of England. The prime minister of the United Kingdom. The president of the United States. It was the Ice Bucket Challenge. It involved taking a bucket of ice water and pouring it over one's head, posting a video of it on social media, and challenging others to do the same. It was done to raise awareness and funds for amyotrophic lateral sclerosis (ALS), also known as Lou Gehrig's disease, a rare motor neuron disease that ultimately leads to the degeneration of muscles and paralysis. There is no cure for ALS yet, and people afflicted with ALS usually die a few years after the onset of initial symptoms.

In the summer of 2014, two young ALS activists, Patrick Quinn and Peter Frates, popularized the Ice Bucket Challenge, which became a viral social media phenomenon. Quinn was afflicted with ALS. The Ice Bucket Challenge led to millions of social media likes and views. More importantly, it raised awareness about ALS, which affects about twenty thousand Americans at any given time,[1] and it raised over $220 million worldwide for ALS research and causes.[2]

The Ice Bucket Challenge is in one way a feel-good story about social media, but in a greater sense it illustrates a larger, unfolding story about activism and technology. The success of the Ice Bucket Challenge in raising both awareness and funds was undoubtedly remarkable. Equally remarkable was the fact that it was done by two ordinary individuals without big budgets or any special connections. Rather, with the use of new information and financial technology, Quinn and Frates were able to translate and amplify their activism nationally and globally with incredible results.

New technology has transformed activism for activists, businesses, and society. New technology like social media and financial technology has both amplified traditional methods and introduced new methods of social activism. Boycotts, marches, and mass protests are now coordinated online among strangers around the world. Hashtag campaigns and viral videos elevate awareness of social issues. Images and videos advocating for social change are now created and broadcasted using social media platforms that reach billions of people across the world for free. As Simon Mainwaring remarked in his book *We First: How Brands and Consumers Use Social Media to Build a Better World*, "the world is witnessing the ability of social media to connect people and spread the ideas, values, and courage needed for significant political and social transformation in several countries."[3]

Furthermore, financial technology has empowered activists and citizens to collect capital and affect the business fortunes of companies in unprecedented ways. Capital for social activism is now frequently raised via crowdfunding and other financial technology platforms capable of reaching a global pool of potential donors and investors almost instantaneously. Hundreds of thousands of dollars can be raised from around the world in a matter of days from the convenience of a phone. Retail investors using memes and trading apps can send a company's stock soaring or plummeting from the convenience of their phones, creating real financial consequences for businesses. Activists can use these new financial technologies to rally support for businesses or register their disapproval of business actions by moving shares in the marketplace like never before. As such, new technology has dramatically changed the means and ends of activism in ways previously unimaginable.

At the same time, the ascent of new technology has also reshaped expectations about corporate social behavior. Consumers, shareholders, and activists can directly engage businesses and business leaders like never before. Moreover, corporate action—and inaction—are scrutinized and analyzed by the masses, affecting corporate brands, business revenue, and market value. This heightened awareness of and attention on corporations has pushed society to challenge previous understandings of the role of businesses. In particular, many now see businesses as more than just amoral vehicles for commerce, sales, and profits. They now see businesses as members of society with obligations beyond those reflected on a balance sheet.

This new blend of activism, capitalism, and technology can marshal millions of people to act on an issue and place significant, direct pressure on businesses and policymakers. This new blended force has changed the power dynamics across many establishments and throughout communities around the world. In their revelatory book *New Power: How Power Works in Our Hyperconnected World—and How to Make It Work for You*, Jeremy Heimans and Henry Timms described this new powerful force as "open, participatory, and peer-driven," and "most powerful when it surges."[4]

In the past, corporate executives feared a bad newspaper story; today, they dread a bad viral video or negative trending hashtag that hurts their brands and stock prices. According to the *New York Times*, "Online campaigns against brands have become one of the most powerful forces in business, giving customers a huge megaphone with which to shape corporate ethics and practices, and imperiling some of the most towering figures of media and industry."[5]

Furthermore, the spotlight generated by these new methods of socioeconomic activism often attracts the attention of policymakers and regulators, who in turn place additional pressure on businesses. For example, the consequential #MeToo movement gained much awareness and momentum online that then translated offline into reforms in business practices. The broad reach and deep impact of social activism powered by new information technology means that businesses are frequently engaged in social issues whether they want to be or not.

The potency of this new cocktail blending activism, capitalism, and technology was made abundantly clear in recent years with the viral videos of Black men and women being killed by police officers, and the ensuing national outrage and mass protests. The tragic and horrific killings of Trayvon Martin, Eric Garner, George Floyd, Breonna Taylor, and so many others in their respective locales would not have been known nationally and internationally without this new interplay of activism and technology. The swift and sustained mass protests that followed would also not have happened as quickly, as loudly, or as forcibly without this new interplay highlighting the longstanding and deadly scourge of racism. Similarly, the subsequent, long-over-due changes in policies and practices from governments and businesses in the cause of racial justice would not have happened with the same kind of urgency without the new powerful symbiosis of activism, capitalism, and technology.

The days of regional social issues staying regional are over. The days of parochial social issues staying confined are over. For companies and executives during this new era of social activism, it means that everything can become their business—from a bathroom bill in North Carolina to the name of a professional football team to the state flag of South Carolina.

BATHROOMS IN NORTH CAROLINA

Bathrooms. It was about bathrooms, and something even more basic.

In March 2016, the state of North Carolina enacted the Public Facilities Privacy & Security Act, better known as House Bill 2 or simply HB2, with the support of then governor Pat McCrory.[6] The law explicitly required transgender individuals to use the public restrooms that corresponded to the biological sex identified on their birth certificate. Additionally, the law explicitly established classes of individuals protected against discrimination in North Carolina and prohibited municipalities from expanding that standard, which excluded members of the LGBTQ community. This meant that even if certain towns or cities in North Carolina wanted to offer more protections and rights to the LGBTQ community, there were legally prohibited from doing so.

Why were bathrooms in public buildings even a subject of legislative debate and action in North Carolina in 2016? According to reporting at the time, proponents of HB2 argued that it was necessary to protect women and children from "potentially dangerous intrusions by biological males."[7] Dan Forest, then lieutenant governor of North Carolina, said, "If our action in keeping men out of women's bathrooms and showers protected the life of just one child or one woman from being molested or assaulted, it was worth it."[8] To be clear, there was no evidence suggesting that people choosing which bathrooms to use for themselves was leading to violence against women or children in the state. Opponents of the law viewed HB2 as state-sanctioned discrimination against the LGBTQ community.

Shortly after HB2 became law, opposition arose swift and strong within North Carolina and beyond. Thousands of people organized and voiced their outrage on social media. Celebrities and businesses also joined in the opposition. Hashtag campaigns like #BoycottNC and #WeAreNotThis were trending on all of the major social media platforms like Twitter, Facebook, and Instagram. Many celebrities, including Bruce Springsteen and Ringo Starr, canceled North Carolina events in protest. The NBA canceled its 2017 All-Star Game in Charlotte, and the NCAA relocated major events, including seven championship events, out of North Carolina due to what it termed "cumulative actions taken by the state concerning civil rights protections."[9] The removal of the NBA All-Star Game and NCAA basketball games were particularly painful for the basketball-loving state.

Prominent businesses, like Apple, Bank of America, Facebook, General Electric, Google, Lyft, Merck, and Starbucks, also joined the effort by publicly opposing HB2. Over two hundred major corporations cosigned a letter with the Human Rights Campaign, the largest LGBTQ advocacy organization in the world, calling for the law's repeal because "HB 2 is not a bill that reflects the values of our companies, of our country, or even the overwhelming majority of North Carolinians."[10] These businesses also lobbied and pressured legislators. PayPal, for instance, said it would scrap plans for a major operations development in North Carolina. Similarly, Deutsche Bank, the investment bank, froze all hiring in North Carolina. The Associated Press estimated that the response to HB2 would cost the state about $3.76 billion in lost business and jobs over a dozen years.[11]

In the face of this potent new form of corporate social activism, Pat McCrory was narrowly voted out of office in November 2016, and in March 2017, HB2 was partially repealed by North Carolina's new governor, Roy Cooper. Despite the repeal of HB2, North Carolina continued to work for years to fix the reputational damage done by the law.

THE WASHINGTON FOOTBALL TEAM

There is a professional football team in Washington, DC. In its illustrious history, it has won three Super Bowls and counts among its veterans numerous Hall of Famers. It is one of the most valuable professional sports franchises in the world, worth in excess of $3 billion.[12] In 2020, its official name was creative and catchy: the Washington Football Team.

As football fans know, from 1933 to 2020 the team was called the Washington Redskins, and the moniker has been controversial for nearly as long. Many found the name and the team's trademarked images to be racist and offensive to Native Americans. For years, Native American and civil rights groups like the National Congress of American Indians and the NAACP pressed for a name change, without success. The team resisted all attempts, insisting the name was an honorific that celebrated the bravery of Native Americans. The NFL and many of the team's fans also supported the Redskins moniker.

In 1999, businessman Daniel Snyder purchased the team for what was then a recording-breaking price of $800 million for a professional sports franchise. One of his first moves as the new owner was to sell the naming rights to the team's home field, Jack Kent Cooke Stadium, which was named after the team's previous longtime owner. Being a true über-capitalist, Snyder sold the stadium rights to the highest bidder, FedEx, for over $200 million.[13]

Dan Snyder tried valiantly to turn his investment in the football team into a winning one, on and off the field, with little success. On the field, he signed expensive free agents and changed head coaches every few years, with little to show for it. During his two-decade-plus tenure, the team has had a losing record, no Super Bowl rings, and a trail of former head coaches. Off the field, Snyder found numerous ways to monetize the team, alienate the fans, and enrich himself. He raised ticket prices, charged for tailgating, sued season ticket holders for late payments, and temporarily banned signs from the stadium.

Snyder was very clear on his position about the team's controversial name. He wanted to keep his team as the Washington Redskins. In 2013, he told a *USA Today* reporter, "We'll never change the name. It's that simple. NEVER—you can use caps."[14] "NEVER" turned out to last only seven years.

During the tumultuous summer of 2020, when the nation was experiencing a new wave of activism around social justice, Snyder announced that the team would no longer be called the Washington Redskins. Starting in July 2020, the team would temporarily be known as the Washington Football Team, pending a new name.

It is hard to say what ultimately led to Snyder's change of heart and change of name, but there are clues. In June 2020, Native American activists persuaded eighty-seven institutional investors and shareholders to send a letter to three of the team's biggest sponsors—Nike, Pepsi, and FedEx—demanding that they sever ties with the team unless it changed its name.[15] The investors were collectively worth $620 billion at the time, and the Redskins' biggest sponsors represented some of the most valuable corporate sponsors of the NFL as well, so this made other teams and the entire league think twice about standing by Snyder and the offensive moniker.[16]

At the same time, the controversy lit up social media, as activists and consumers engaged on the issue and the larger challenges of social justice in America, particularly for African Americans and other minorities in this country. People organized online and on the streets. The name of the professional football team in Washington became more than just a local issue for fans of the team. It was now a national issue splashed across newspaper headlines and hotly debated by sports fans and nonfans alike. Businesses took notice and responded in kind. In early July, FedEx wrote a letter demanding the team change its name, and Nike stopped selling Redskins apparel on its website.[17]

A few days later, Snyder made his announcement about the name change.

THE CONFEDERATE FLAG

There were Black churches in America before we even became a country. Slaves organized churches in present-day South Carolina and Georgia before they were freed, and before we as colonies broke free from the tyranny of Great Britain.

Mother Emanuel, the Emanuel African Methodist Episcopal Church in Charleston, South Carolina, was organized in 1817; it is part of the rich lineage of Black churches in America. For centuries, it has served as a refuge for slaves, freed people, and their sons and daughters—through the horrors of slavery, the lash of Jim Crow, the struggles for change, and the promise and realization of progress.

On Wednesday evening, June 17, 2015, thirteen people attended Bible study at Mother Emanuel. Only four of them would leave alive. The session was led by Reverend Clementa Pinckney, the senior pastor of the church who was also state senator. Among the thirteen people in attendance that evening was a young man named Dylann Roof who had driven to the church from North Carolina. Shortly after the start of Bible study, Roof opened fire on the other participants and massacred nine people with whom he had prayed just moments before.

Roof, it turned out, was a white supremacist who wanted to start a race war. He drove hundreds of miles to Charleston to kill African Americans. Investigators discovered his hateful online postings filled with neo-Nazi and white supremacist imagery. Chief among them were images with the Confederate flag.

In the aftermath of the shooting, families of the victims gracefully forgave Roof for his heinous act, and President Barack Obama memorably eulogized, in word and song, the nine African American victims and their amazing grace.

Behind the scenes after the massacre, there was a movement to get then governor Nikki Haley to remove the flag from state capitol grounds. The Confederate flag for many was a symbol of racism, bigotry, and a dark defeated past being revised as glorious in the present. For many, it was a hateful symbol too often misappropriated by white supremacists longing to return to the days of a segregated South. For others, the flag was a symbol of Southern heritage and tradition.

This movement to remove the flag from the state capitol was not a new one. In 2000, the state had fiercely debated the issue. Passions on both sides ran strong and steadfast. Politicians, particularly those in the South, were reluctant to condemn or acknowledge the hurt the flag caused to many people, particularly African Americans, for fear of alienating voters and constituencies in the South who viewed the flag positively. Even a politically brave maverick—Senator John McCain—was reluctant to condemn the Confederate flag in South Carolina during his 2000 run for the Republican presidential nomination against George W. Bush. To McCain's credit, he later returned to South Carolina and publicly apologized for not expressing his true views about the flag as "a symbol of racism and slavery," and he called for its removal from the top of the statehouse in Charleston.[18]

After much heated debate about heritage, hate, history, state's rights, the past, and the present, in May 2000 South Carolina passed a law to move the flag from the top of the statehouse dome to the front of the Capitol with a Confederate monument. The law was a compromise that did not satisfy many on either side of the issue.

The shooting at Mother Emanuel and the shooter's affinity for the Confederate flag reignited the Confederate flag controversy. While much had changed in South Carolina, and in the country as a whole, in the fifteen years since the flag was removed from the top of the statehouse little about the competing perspectives had actually changed. It remained a tough issue for elected officials in the South. The mere suggestion of removing the flag from the Capitol's grounds led to death threats against Governor Haley.

However, unlike in 2000, the eyes of the nation were on South Carolina, and many Americans across the country made their views directly known to Haley on social media both in opposition and in support of the flag. The governor received thousands of messages directly or indirectly via Facebook, Twitter, and Instagram. As part of a new generation of social media–savvy politicians, Haley was acutely aware of how many people around her state and the country stood in opposition to the Confederate flag.

Moreover, many major businesses openly opposed the flag and urged Governor Haley to take action on the issue. Amazon and Walmart, the two largest retailers in the country, announced that they would ban the sale of items bearing the Confederate flag. Other companies—like Boeing, which had a significant and growing presence in South Carolina—publicly urged the governor to remove the flag from the state capitol grounds. Haley had worked hard during her tenure to rebrand South Carolina as business-friendly, so she was particularly sensitive to business reactions on the issues.

On July 15, 2015, Governor Haley ordered that the Confederate flag be moved from the state capitol grounds to the South Carolina Confederate Relic Room and Military Museum.

In the years that followed, other states and municipalities wrestled with the controversy surrounding the Confederate flag and other Confederate monuments. Perhaps most surprising, in 2020, in the wake of a season of protests for racial justice, Mississippi passed a law that would not only remove its state flag—whose design incorporated the Confederate battle flag—but also replace it with an entirely new flag. Again, the forces that succeeded in removing and replacing the Mississippi state flag were a combination of activists and capitalists amplified by new media and financial technology working to bring down a flag that had flown defiantly in Mississippi for more than a century.

THE TIMES THEY ARE A-CHANGIN'

In each of these episodes, activists working with businesses, using new media and consumer technology, brought about progress in a status quo that until then had seemed immovable.

These episodes are now the norm in activism, not the exception, and not just in the United States but around the world. For instance, Swedish teenage climate activist Greta Thunberg leveraged social media to organize an international student strike from school to raise awareness and demand action on climate change. Her efforts were supported by many business executives and garnered her numerous accolades, including *Time* magazine's Person of the Year and number one *New York Times* best-selling author. Given the grassroots nature of modern corporate social activism, her book was appropriately titled *No One Is Too Small to Make a Difference.*[19]

Undoubtedly, the moment in time—the historical context, the social zeitgeist, and the earlier foundation laid by others—for each of these episodes served as incubators for this new corporate social activism as well. Nevertheless, it is hard to argue against the notion that activists or capitalists alone could have done what they did together had they been working separately and without the tools of modern technology. Technology helped to change and amplify these issues and causes. The lonely soloist became part of a boisterous choir as the cause of individual activists became a movement. Traditionally local issues became national issues. The cause of activists became the cause of capitalists. And through shared purpose and common effort, progress was made real.

CHAPTER 5

Restraining a President

THE PRESIDENT RANTED AND RAVED. He was paranoid about a cabal of big media conglomerates, the political establishment, and his aides conspiring against him. He was working with the Russian leadership to tear down traditional American alliances in Europe. He had ideas about using the FBI and the full resources of the federal government to go after his perceived enemies. Our legislative and judicial branches struggled to rein in the most powerful man in the world.

This is not a summary of a recent presidential administration. Rather, it is the plot of a best-selling 1965 novel, *Night of Camp David*, by Fletcher Knebel. The book was reissued in 2018 as political pundits noted its frightening echoes of the Trump administration.[1] The reissued edition had a cover with a simple, ominous question, "What would happen if the president of the U.S.A. went stark raving mad?"

During the Trump campaign and administration spanning over four years, much of the United States went mad. Norms of American politics and common decency were breached. Neighbor turned against neighbor. Name calling and bullying tactics of bad schoolyards became common in the august halls of high office. Perennial dark voices and misguided views that had been dwindling and pushed to the fringes of society by decades of progress found daylight once again. Truth and facts melted from solid into air. Science and data gave way to conspiracies and fiction. Perhaps most distressing during this period was the seeming lack of serious and strong restraints on then president Trump—the lack of checks and willingness to speak truth to power.

The founders of the American system established a system of checks and balances among three branches of government with separated powers, whereby no single person or branch would be dominant. The founders recognized that flawed, self-interested human beings could misuse and abuse their power once in high office, so they designed a system that leverages the flaws and ambitions of humans to serve as protective mechanisms against abuse. As James Madison wrote in Federalist Paper 51:

> Ambition must be made to counteract ambition.
> The interest of the man must be connected with the
> constitutional rights of the place. It may be a reflec-
> tion on human nature, that such devices should
> be necessary to control the abuses of government.
> But what is government itself, but the greatest of all
> reflections on human nature? If men were angels,
> no government would be necessary. If angels were
> to govern men, neither external nor internal con-
> trols on government would be necessary.[2]

Unfortunately, partisan politics and personal ambitions largely thwarted the plans of the founders, particularly in the last few decades. Instead of the executive and legislative branches working to check and balance one another's worst impulses, they now work in concert when they are controlled by the same party and in obstruction when they are controlled by different parties. The judiciary has also grown more partisan as judicial appointments, particularly on the federal appellate courts and the Supreme Court, are either confirmed or rejected based largely along partisan lines.

Instead of a separation of powers, we have a "separation of parties."[3]

This separation of parties has meant that the parties distanced themselves from one another toward their extremes. Cooperation across the aisle was punished within party ranks and by voters in an increasingly polarized country fragmented by gerrymandered districts. Obstruction was rewarded with greater party support (read: money) and re-election. This has created vicious cycles of polarization. As Ezra Klein observed in his definitive tome on polarization in the United States, *Why We're Polarized*:

> Institutions polarize to appeal to a more polarized
> public, which further polarizes the public, which
> forces the institutions to polarize further, and so
> on. Polarization isn't something that happened to
> American politics. It's something that's happening
> to American politics. And it's getting worse.[4]

As the parties became more polarized, the country was left in the abyss, as short-term issues and longer-term systemic problems festered despite the existence of common sense, widely agreed-upon solutions. In recent years, public approval of Congress has hovered around 15 percent, and public laws passed per session have been near all-time lows in the post–World War II period.[5] This hyperpartisanship has led to dysfunction in the government, dissatisfaction in the electorate, and despair in the public.

On June 16, 2015, down a faux-gold escalator, businessman Donald Trump descended into this American political crucible of dysfunction and dissatisfaction and found an even lower level. Right from the start, during his presidential announcement speech, he disparaged Mexican immigrants and migrants as "people that have lots of problems" and "rapists" who are "bringing crime and drugs" into the country.[6]

Initially, Trump was not taken seriously as a candidate by either the media or his opponents in the Republican primary field. They denounced, half-heartedly, his outlandish and offensive statements but figured he stood no chance of winning the nomination, let alone the presidency. He attacked the media, mocked his opponents, and told half-truths and blatant falsehoods. His wild antics gave him more free media coverage with each passing day, and his support grew. As each primary opponent fell to the wayside in the face of his no-holds-barred, professional wrestling–style politics, he improbably won the party of Lincoln's nomination in 2016, and went on to defeat Hillary Clinton in the electoral college to become the president of the United States.

It is one thing to denounce a presidential candidate; it is quite another thing to denounce the president, especially one with a loyal base of supporters. Rather than denounce and restrain him, the Republican Party saw him as an inelegant vehicle for their aspirations of lower taxes, less regulation, and conservative judges. They were willing to ride the tiger, if it took them to their desired destinations. As such, despite the built-in checks and balances of our system of government, there were little restraints on then president Trump.

In the absence of political restraints, activists went online and took to the streets in record numbers numerous times in response to the actions of the Trump administration. More remarkably, some of the most prominent capitalists from the biggest businesses around the country also joined in the activism as many CEOs spoke out against some of the administration's policies. While President Trump ignored the calls of Speaker Nancy Pelosi or other Democrats, as his party stayed largely silent, the CEOs of corporate America got his attention, as he has long fashioned himself a fellow titan of industry.

In an era of unprecedented political dissatisfaction and dysfunction, people turned away from their political leaders and institutions and to businesses and business leaders to help them solve society's most problematic policies and issues. In a 2021 study, a majority of those surveyed saw businesses as the only trusted, ethical, and competent institutions; and 86 percent of respondents expected CEOs to engage in social activism to address the challenges confronting society.[7]

This new social activism from the corner office suites of corporate America did not always seem straightforward or comfortable, as the same companies denouncing some administration policies were also the ones lobbying the administration for lower taxes and less regulation. Nevertheless, this new form of corporate social activism that brought together activists on Main Street and capitalists on Wall Street found a louder and lasting voice during the four years of the Trump administration, from the Muslim ban at the beginning of the term to the failed insurrection that ended it.

THE MUSLIM BAN

In December 2015, presidential candidate Donald Trump called for "a total and complete shutdown of Muslims entering the United States until our country's representatives can figure out what the hell is going on."[8]

In January 2017, about a week after coming into office, President Donald Trump signed Executive Order 13,769, colloquially referred to as the "Trump travel ban," which ostensibly made candidate Trump's call for a Muslim ban official U.S. policy.

The executive order, formally titled "Protecting the Nation from Foreign Terrorist Entry into the United States," suspended the U.S. Refugees Admissions Program and banned entry into the country by people from Iran, Iraq, Libya, Somalia, Sudan, Syria, and Yemen. It was revised by subsequent executive orders after numerous concerns were raised about the hastily drafted initial order. Supporters deemed it necessary for national security to ban citizens of these predominantly Muslim countries. Opponents deemed it a discriminatory "Muslim ban" that ran counter to core American values of tolerance, acceptance, and diversity, to say nothing of the nearly 3.5 million Muslim Americans that called America home.[9]

Politically, little could be done to restrain the executive order. The Republican Party largely supported the executive action with public statements or silent complicity. The Democrats, with no control over Congress, had no meaningful political tools to stop it.

Shortly after Trump issued the executive order, in the absence of political means, opponents organized protests online, in the streets, and in the courts. Because the executive order was issued so hastily and without proper planning and coordination, thousands of Muslims, including citizens and permanent residents of the United States, were left stranded at airports across the country. Thousands gathered at airports around the country to protest and assist those who were detained because of the order. At the behest of the American Civil Liberties Union (ACLU), a federal judge in New York granted a temporary injunction stalling the deportation of Muslims at U.S. airports who were impacted by the order. For its efforts, online donations poured into the ACLU, which garnered about $24 million in donations the weekend the order was signed, a sum greater than all of its donations in 2016.[10]

While the protests happened in the streets, airports, and courts, activists also took the battles online. They waged social media campaigns against the ban immediately, and continued for months afterward. Hashtags like #NoBanNoWall, #Immigrants-Welcome, #RefugeesWelcome, and #NoMuslimBan trended across Twitter, then president's Trump's favorite medium of communication. Online boycott campaigns also targeted Trump-branded products and affiliated companies. Organizations like Grab Your Wallet posted a running tally of companies affiliated with Trump and his businesses. Furthermore, companies perceived as sympathetic to the ban also felt the power of this new high-tech form of social activism. Uber, for instance, was the target of the #DeleteUber campaign, as many saw the company as sympathetic to the Trump administration for providing service to certain airports despite other ride services suspending service in opposition to the ban.[11]

In addition to the expected actions of activists, many major corporations and CEOs publicly spoke out and demonstrated against the ban in an unprecedented fashion. Sergey Brin, Google's cofounder, joined protests at San Francisco International Airport. Netflix CEO Reed Hastings stated that "Trump's actions are hurting Netflix employees around the world, and are so un-American it pains us all. Worse, these actions will make

America less safe (through hatred and loss of allies) rather than more safe."[12] Howard Schultz, then the CEO of Starbucks, wrote a letter to employees announcing plans to hire ten thousand refugees.[13] More than one hundred leading tech firms, including Amazon, Facebook, and Google, jointly filed an amicus brief in a lawsuit against the order, and pledged millions of dollars to aid activists in the fight against the ban.

As a coda, in the summer of 2018, the U.S. Supreme Court upheld the validity of one of the subsequently amended travel ban orders. However, this important initial episode involving the Trump Muslim ban foreshadowed the new vehicle of social change that is corporate social activism, as a check against the most powerful person in the world.

CHARLOTTESVILLE

On Sunday, April 9, 1865, Confederate General Robert E. Lee surrendered to Union General Ulysses S. Grant at the Appomattox Courthouse in Virginia, and thus formally brought the U.S. Civil War to an end. The surrender at Appomattox may have ended serious fighting between the Confederacy and the Union, but it did not end the fight for many sympathizers of the Confederacy.

On Friday, August 11, 2017, the modern heirs to the Confederacy congregated in Charlottesville, Virginia, for a "Unite the Right" rally to defend the honor of General Lee, or rather, the honor of a statue of Lee that it was proposed would be removed from a local park. White nationalists, neo-Nazis, neofascists, Klansmen, and right-wing militias gathered and marched through the bucolic University of Virginia campus carrying burning torches, assault weapons, the Confederate battle flag, the Nazi flag, and other emblems of hate. They chanted racist, anti-Semitic, and bigoted messages, like "You will not replace us!" and "Jews will not replace us!" and "White Lives Matter!" The fire from their torches paled in comparison to the heat from the hate in their eyes and faces. It was like a scene out of a dystopic alternate history film where many of the villains preferred costumes of khakis and polo shirts.

These hateful demonstrators did not have free rein on the streets of Charlottesville. They were met by counterprotestors, police, and media. The violent protests and confrontations became deadly on the second day, Saturday, August 12, when a white nationalist drove a car into a crowd, injuring some and killing Heather Heyer, a young woman peacefully protesting against hate in her community; two police officers near the scene died in a helicopter crash.[14] Governor Terry McAuliffe declared a state of emergency and put an end to the hate-filled rally later that day.

In the days that followed, it took President Trump numerous attempts to issue a strong condemnation of the hate-filled posse of demonstrators. Initially, Trump spoke out against the violence and blamed "many sides" for the disturbance.[15] There was much outcry after this statement, as many felt that Trump was suggesting a moral equivalence between the white nationalists and those protesting them. In subsequent statements, Trump said "You also had people that were very fine people, on both sides."[16] Again, on one side were neo-Nazis and Klansmen and on the other side were people protesting them, made up largely of faith-based organizations, Black Lives Matter, and other peaceful social activists.

Following his statements, the president was roundly condemned in the media. Politically, Democrats and a few Republicans like Senators John McCain and Jeff Flake forcefully condemned the president. Again, many in his party remained silent or tepid in their condemnation as the president continued to pay no political consequence for his hurtful statements.

While the activists and politicians were unable to get the president's attention, one small group had more success—the CEOs of America's largest companies. Executives, like the CEOs of Merck and Under Armour, publicly rebuked the president for his statements and resigned from various presidential advisory councils. Executives on the White House's elite Strategic and Policy Forum, as well as those on the Manufacturing Jobs Initiative, convened multiple calls that resulted in the executives resigning en masse from those two councils. These executives are some of the foremost business leaders in the world, representing companies like Pepsi, JPMorgan Chase, General Electric, IBM, and Walmart. But before the executives could publicly announce their mass protest resignation, President Trump disbanded both councils—in a tweet.

To be sure, the actions of these corporate executives did not miraculously change Trump's outlook or behavior, but they certainly got his attention and gave him some pause, because he understood the language of capital and commerce, if not of traditional politics and activism.

SEPARATED FAMILIES AND CAGED CHILDREN

President Trump campaigned on a strong "America first" immigration policy. The execution of his immigration policies led to separated families and caged children.

In September 2017, President Trump announced plans to end the Obama administration's Deferred Action for Childhood Arrivals (DACA) program, purportedly to protect Americans and American jobs from illegal immigrants. DACA allowed undocumented immigrants who were brought into the country as children to remain and work in the country without the specter of deportation. At the time of the announcement, approximately eight hundred thousand young people were protected by DACA.[17] These individuals were Americans in everything but documentation. They were raised here, educated here, worked here, and lived here as fully as any other American. Yet because of the termination of DACA, hundreds of thousands of people could be separated from their families and deported to a "homeland" that was completely foreign to them. And many were.

A few months after ending DACA, the Trump administration continued to push its hardline immigration policy. In early 2018, Attorney General Jeff Sessions announced a zero-tolerance policy for unauthorized entries into the United States from its Southern border.[18] As part of the new policy, children who entered the country illegally would be separated from their parents or relatives and placed in cages in different holding facilities. Some of these children were so young that they were still in diapers.

The Trump administration saw the family separation and caging of children as an effective tool for deterring illegal immigration. This is despite the fact that many of these migrants were refugees looking for safe harbor in America after a long, perilous journey without adequate food or water. White House Chief of Staff John Kelly said at the time, "They're coming here for a reason. And I sympathize with the reason. But the laws are the laws. But a big name of the game is deterrence."[19]

To make matters worse, the administration did not have an orderly process for reunifying the separated children from their families. As a result, hundreds of children would remain separated from their families and live years of their youth inside cages in a U.S. detention facility. For Attorney General Jeff

Sessions, the blame for the plight of the separated and orphaned children rested with their parents: "If people don't want to be separated from their children, they should not bring them with them. We've got to get this message out."[20]

Echoing the response to the previous controversial acts of the administration, many Republicans supported the DACA decision and the hardline, zero-tolerance immigration policy, as it reflected the fervent views of their base. Democrats' protests fell on the deaf ears of the administration. Again, the traditional levers of politics failed on one issue—immigration—about which a majority of Americans wanted sensible, humane reforms.

Just as with previous controversial actions of the Trump administration, the outcry against ending DACA and the hardline family separation policy was strong and swift. Activists went online and into the streets in the tens of thousands across the country to protest. Lawyers filed suits in courts to block the administration's actions.

And again, corporate executives joined the activists' cause to try to restrain the most powerful person in the world. CEOs like Mark Zuckerberg of Facebook and Tim Cook of Apple publicly condemned the actions and vowed to fight for the immigrants affected by DACA. After the rescission of DACA, Zuckerberg stated, "It is particularly cruel to offer young people the American dream, encourage them to come out of the shadows and trust our government, and then punish them for it."[21] Hundreds of business leaders also wrote an open letter to the president and congressional leaders, imploring them to act on behalf of the young people affected by DACA. They did the same for the hardline family separation policy. These titans of industry would join their voices, prestige, and resources with the efforts of activists to try to bring about change where the process of government had failed.

In part as a result of this wave of corporate social activism and the bad press coverage it helped engender, the Trump administration lost several lawsuits, including one in the U.S. Supreme Court on DACA, and President Trump issued a new executive order to end the family separation policy.

THE FAILED INSURRECTION

After nearly four tumultuous and consequential years, President Trump lost his reelection bid to Vice President Joe Biden. Rather than graciously concede the election and begin a peaceful transition like almost every one of his predecessors, Trump engaged in an unprecedented, prolonged effort to overturn the presidential election, which led to a failed insurrection on the U.S. Capitol.

In the 2020 election, during a pandemic that was killing thousands of people each day, Americans turned out to vote in record numbers. And largely because of the pandemic, a record number of Americans voted early and voted by mail. Because of these unusual circumstances, the election results were not known on election night, Tuesday, November 3, 2020, as millions of votes were still being tabulated. By Saturday, November 7, 2020, major television networks and the Associated Press called the presidential race for Biden.

Instead of conceding, Trump and his supporters claimed, without providing any real evidence, that there was massive voter fraud and that the election had been stolen from him. In the ensuing weeks, as each state legislature certified its election results, Trump and his supporters pressured state legislators and election officials to overturn the will of the people and disenfranchise millions of voters. Fortunately, these efforts on the state level failed as each state certified its results in accordance with the tallied votes.

On January 6, 2021, Congress convened, with Vice President Mike Pence presiding over the session, to count and certify each state's electoral college votes, as required under the Constitution. In a last-gasp effort, Trump spent the days preceding the certification pressuring Pence to overturn the election result, even though the vice president does not possess that legal power.

On January 6, Trump and his supporters gathered at a "Save America" rally, hoping to intimidate members of Congress to object and deny the final certification of the election results. The speakers at the rally again riled up the crowd of Trump supporters with baseless claims of a fraudulent and stolen election. Trump urged his supporters to "fight like hell" and "walk down to the Capitol" and "show strength" to Congress. Thousands of supporters marched toward the Capitol, overpowered the police, tore down barricades, scaled walls, and entered the Capitol as Congress was moving to certify the election. Once inside, this band of marauders ransacked the hallowed halls of Congress, stole documents, vandalized property, and injured numerous police officers. They entered the Senate and House Chambers seeking to harm Pence and other officials like Speaker Pelosi.

During the insurrection, President Trump reportedly watched without concern from the comfort of the White House. After pressure from his senior staff, Trump put out a video calling the rioters "very special people" and asking them to "go home in peace."

Hours later, the insurrection ended, quelled by the National Guard. Congress returned late in the evening and ultimately certified Joe Biden as the president-elect of the United States. Yet even after the insurrection, over a hundred House Republicans and a handful of senators, namely Senators Ted Cruz and Josh Hawley, objected to the certification of the election results from the states.

Five people died as a result of this failed insurrection.

In the days that followed, a stunned nation and world watched as the president continued to refuse to explicitly concede the election. And again, many in his party refused to condemn him.

In a surprising move, many of America's largest corporations spoke out openly and strongly against the insurrection and temporarily suspended campaign contributions, particularly to elected officials who had attempted to overturn the election. Hundreds of companies, like Airbnb, Microsoft, Walmart, and the Walt Disney Company, paused political contributions in response to the failed insurrection. Not surprisingly, this got the attention of the elected officials, as the oxygen for the campaigns was suddenly turned off.

Most significantly, social media companies like Twitter, Facebook, and YouTube suspended President Trump from their platforms. According to multiple reports, the ban from Twitter deeply angered Trump, as it deprived him of his preferred megaphone of communication to his fervent followers and the world. Additionally, many high-profile businesses and law firms severed their ties to Trump-affiliated business after the failed insurrection. Notably, the PGA took away the 2022 PGA Championship previous scheduled for Trump National Golf Club in Bedminster, New Jersey. This PGA's decision reportedly greatly upset President Trump, an avid golfer and fan of the game.

In the waning days of Trump's presidency, he was impeached an unprecedented second time, and President Joe Biden was sworn in on Wednesday, January 20, 2021. About a month later, Trump was acquitted in the Senate, with fifty-seven guilty votes and forty-three not guilty votes, failing to meet the constitutional threshold of sixty-seven votes for a conviction, even though it was the most bipartisan impeachment vote in history.

A NEW POLITICS OF BUSINESS

The four years of the Trump administration brought incredibly damaging tumult and chaos to the country during a period of political dysfunction and dangerous hyperpartisanship. The world saw firsthand what can happen when the most powerful man in the world operates with little to no governmental checks. Undoubtedly, the forces unleashed or resurfaced by former president Trump and his supporters will continue to animate and influence American politics. That said, the four years of the Trump administration also awakened a new sense of activism and civic duty in this country, which will also continue to animate and influence American politics. It gave birth to a new sense of politics and civics in America.

People of all ages and from all classes, creeds, and backgrounds engaged in protests for the first time in the name of racial justice, environment protection, democracy, and the rule of law. And businesses were moved by the actions of the people—the same people that were their customers, employees, shareholders, and fellow citizens—to speak out and act against social injustice. While the legacy of the four years of the Trump presidency remains to be written, one important chapter in the first draft should be about the rise of the new force for social progress that united activists and capitalists to work together when our elected officials were unwilling or unable to check and restrain abuses of power. Whether that new force will be used in a consistent and sustained fashion remains to be seen, but that force has been undeniably awakened.

CHAPTER 6

Original Sins

OR A VERY BRIEF PERIOD IN 2019, due to a clerical error at the U.S. Department of Agriculture, the Kingdom of Wakanda was a free trade partner of the United States.[1] Wakanda is the fictional East African homeland of Marvel Comics superhero Black Panther, aka T'Challa. As depicted in the 2018 blockbuster movie *Black Panther*, starring the late Chadwick Boseman, Wakanda was a vibrant kingdom with an abundance of wealth, advanced technology, natural resources, and powerful, smart Black leaders.

Wakanda is not real, but nearly a century before the movie, there was a place like Wakanda in America. It was the Greenwood District of Tulsa, Oklahoma, during the oil boom of the early 1900s, home to a brilliant African American professional class of lawyers, bankers, doctors, and engineers. Greenwood was known as Black Wall Street. It was a thriving community where African Americans owned most of the businesses during a time of segregation in most of the country.

Greenwood's prosperity came to an abrupt and horrific end on Memorial Day weekend 1921 in what would become known as the Tulsa Race Massacre. On Tuesday, May 31, 1921, Dick Rowland, a young Black man, was arrested for allegedly assaulting Sarah Page, a young white woman. The accusation and charges were in dispute from the start and remained just as disputed in 2001 when Oklahoma issued its final report on the Massacre.[2]

Later that Tuesday, rumors that Rowland would be lynched spread throughout Tulsa. The talk of a lynching attracted an angry and armed white mob of hundreds to the local courthouse. A smaller group of Black men, intent on preventing a lynching of one of their own, showed up armed at the courthouse as well.

As the dueling mobs and crowds gathered tensely at the courthouse that evening, a single shot was fired. That shot would trigger countless more, aimed mostly and indiscriminately at the Black residents of Greenwood. In addition to the gunfights, fires were set to the Black-owned businesses in the wee hours of Wednesday, June 1, 1921. In the course of less than two days, Greenwood was destroyed. An estimated forty blocks of businesses and homes were decimated. Thousands were injured, and hundreds died. The following day the National Guard came in and put an end to the unrest.

Rather than offering redress or support, white local officials and citizens systematically erased the massacre from history. All-white juries refused to indict most of the perpetrators. And those who were indicted were not convicted of any serious charges against them. No compensation was ever offered for the lost lives and destroyed property. The erasure and cover-up were so complete that for decades very few people knew about

Black Wall Street or how it had been destroyed in two days. It was not acknowledged or taught locally in schools for decades, and rarely mentioned nationally.

On the ninetieth anniversary of the incident in 2011, the *New York Times* called the event "what may be the deadliest occurrence of racial violence in United States history—an episode so brutal that this city, in a bout of collective amnesia that extended more than a half-century, simply chose to forget it ever happened. The Tulsa race riot of 1921 was rarely mentioned in history books, classrooms or even in private. Blacks and whites alike grew into middle age unaware of what had taken place."[3]

Oklahoma did not officially or truly acknowledge the event until 2001, when the 1921 Tulsa Race Riot Reconciliation Act was signed into law. Nevertheless, ignorance and silence among the general public about the horrors that occurred in Greenwood remained the norm for nearly a century. In 2021, during the hundredth anniversary of the massacre, a changing nation finally became more aware of what happened in Tulsa, as national and local press widely covered the once suppressed dark chapter in American history. President Joe Biden even marked the event by giving a moving speech in Tulsa to, in his words, "fill the silence."

The history of the 1921 Tulsa Race Massacre and its aftermath tells a story of both tragedy and resilience in the long struggle for racial justice in America. The facts of Tulsa are not unique in America's past or present on matters of race. The false accusation, the lack of real due process, the racially motivated brutality, the institutional suppression, and the absence of meaningful government acknowledgment and action are tragically all too common. But so too are the resilience and the strength of the people: to struggle, to survive, and to thrive in the face of overwhelming odds.

While significant progress has been made on matters of racial justice and equality, the stains and pains of what

President Barack Obama called our "nation's original sin of slavery" still shackles and stifles America as a nation.[4] Hard-fought and hard-won progress on civil rights seems to be easily weakened and stripped away by a new executive action, state law, or court ruling. For many, exceptional Black standouts often seem unfairly just that, the exception and not the norm. Too many Black communities and families have been left behind in the growth and progress of America. Intergenerational wealth and capital accumulation still remain elusive for too many. Many uneven and unfair structures of systemic racism seem to have mutated into forms even stronger and more difficult to dismantle. And making it all worse is the inability or unwillingness of too many of our political leaders and institutions to address matters of race—or to address it in an honest, nuanced, and constructive fashion, given all of the raw histories, complexities, and emotions that it engenders.

There is no easy approach to untying or cutting the Gordian knot that is race in America. No one person or institution can do it, but activists and capitalists working together, thoughtfully and empathetically, might be able to loosen it. And by doing so might help make new and creative approaches more workable on matters of race, gender, and other endemic issues that have entangled and ensnared so much of American history and American life.

THE HARD BUSINESS OF RACE

Eight minutes and forty-six seconds. A horrific cause of death. A rallying cry of protest. A cruel marker of time in a long struggle.

Eight minutes and forty-six seconds. According to prosecutors, this was the amount of time George Floyd spent with his neck under the knee of a police officer before he died. On camera. In broad daylight. In the presence of other police officers. In front of witnesses. In America. In 2020.

Actually, the prosecutor was imprecise about the time. Subsequent video analysis suggests that the time Floyd spent under the knee of the officer was closer to nine and a half minutes.[5]

Mr. Floyd was being arrested for allegedly using a counterfeit bill in Minneapolis, Minnesota, on Monday, May 25, 2020, when he was killed. Derek Chauvin, a Minneapolis police officer, planted his knee on Floyd's neck against the pavement during the arrest. Mr. Floyd gasped for breath. He repeatedly called for his mother and said, "I can't breathe." A jury would later convict Chauvin of murdering Floyd; and a judge would sentence him to 22.5 years in prison.

A smartphone video of the killing of George Floyd made by seventeen-year-old Darnella Frazier was viewed millions of times on social media. It sparked a wave of global protests in the days and weeks that followed. Thousands of American towns and cities saw mass demonstrations in the midst of a global pandemic. In numerous cities, the protests turned violent when a few rioters and looters upended what were largely peaceful demonstrations, leading to clashes with police personnel. Many cities imposed curfews, and numerous governors activated their respective National Guard troops to quell the unrest. Fires, smoke, tear gas, flash grenades, broken glass, smashed store fronts, boarded-up windows, and police in riot gear became a common scene on television and news reports across America.

This extraordinary outpouring of outrage and protest was not just for George Floyd but for centuries of wrongs against the Black community in America. Wrongs whose prevalence seems not to diminish with the passage of time, but actually worsen in the eyes of many. The killing of George Floyd came on the heels of killings of African Americans by the police. Killings that made names like Trayvon Martin, Michael Brown, Breonna Taylor, Ahmaud Arbery, and Eric Garner familiar in a long, unfolding American tragedy with countless unknown names; countless sons and daughters who met the same cruel, premature end.

Floyd's killing came in the midst of a movement for racial justice known as Black Lives Matter, which was initiated in the aftermath of the acquittal of George Zimmerman for fatally shooting Trayvon Martin, an innocent teenager. The movement was decentralized, with activists around the world working toward the shared goal of racial justice through demonstrations, protests, and discussions, both online and offline. Black Lives Matter became not just the name of a movement but a powerful reminder of the stain and pain of one of America's original sins.

The dysfunction of the federal government was evident again when the nation was crying out for action on racial violence and systemic racism, as Congress failed to take any meaningful action in the aftermath of Floyd's killing and the mass demonstrations. In early 2021, an antilynching bill, the Emmett Till Antilynching Act, named for a fourteen-year-old Black boy who was lynched in Mississippi in 1955, failed to advance to become law, despite overwhelming bipartisan support, because one Republican senator had objections to some language in the bill.

In the absence of meaningful government policy action, the killing of Floyd and the ensuing protests moved many businesses and business leaders to take new action on issues of racial justice and equality in the weeks and months that followed. As expected, many businesses denounced racism, and pledged to increase diversity in their ranks, promote antiracism training, and donate money and expertise to civil rights and activist organizations working on matters of racial justice. Many businesses also started initiatives to work on racial justice with activist organizations.

More significantly, many businesses pledged and acted more expansively and creatively to address the various social barriers of racism. Venture capital firms Andreessen Horowitz and Soft-Bank started funds for entrepreneurs from underrepresented and underserved communities. Apple created a camp for Black coders and computer engineers to help increase minority representation in technology. Sephora and many other national retailers took the 15 Percent Pledge to source 15 percent of their product offerings from Black-owned businesses. Target, based in Floyd's hometown of Minneapolis, created a consulting service to help Black-owned, local small businesses after the unrest in the city. Viacom and WarnerMedia each started initiatives to fund and air more social justice content on various platforms. The NASDAQ adopted a rule requiring that their listing companies have at least two diverse directors, or explain their failure to comply.

Some of the most expansive, creative, and perhaps most impactful corporate actions were those related to finance. Netflix, for instance, pledged to move $100 million or 2 percent of its cash equivalents to banks that work primarily with Black communities.[6] Most large companies like Netflix usually keep their accounts with giant financial institutions and not Black community banks and credit unions. This simple but pathbreaking transfer of a small portion of its cash would give notoriously undercapitalized Black banks more capital for lending and serving their communities.

On a larger and more comprehensive scale, JPMorgan Chase made a $30 billion commitment to help promote racial equity and close the racial wealth gap.[7] As part of this huge commitment, it would fund minority depository institutions (MDIs) and diverse-led community development financial institutions (CDFIs) with the creation of a new type of securities through a partnership with Google.[8] It would also make direct investments and give tax credits to MDIs and CDFIs that serve predominantly Black communities and Black clienteles. By funding these Black financial institutions, they make it easier for Black entrepreneurs and citizens to find capital and build wealth.

While corporate initiatives in finance might not be as high profile and social media friendly as other actions—like painting "Black Lives Matter" in giant block letters on the streets of U.S. cities—they can have a tremendous, lasting impact on curbing the injustices of systemic racism when designed and implemented thoughtfully. This is especially true when smart business programs targeting systemic racism are coupled with sensible government actions that address the longstanding, underlying structural problems in a meaningful way. Nevertheless, it is important to emphasize that impactful private action alone, through businesses working within flawed economic systems and structures stained with the dark legacy of racial discrimination, will not be enough to undo generations of misdeeds.

Mehrsa Baradaran, in her magisterial book *The Color of Money: Black Banks and the Racial Wealth Gap*, highlighted how historical systemic racism in finance and banking blocked generations of African Americans from creating and building lasting wealth: "Housing segregation, racism, and Jim Crow credit policies create an inescapable economic trap for Black communities and their banks. Black banking has been an anemic response to racial inequality that has yielded virtually nothing in closing the wealth gap."[9]

While the country has gotten wealthier as a whole, the racial wealth gap has not really moved in more than half a century between Black and white households.[10] Black homeownership is around 40 percent, while white homeownership is around 73 percent.[11] This is startling and deeply concerning, because homeownership is one of the critical ways to create lasting wealth.

Beyond homeownership, Black workers are twice as likely to be unemployed compared to their white counterparts, in addition to being paid, on average, nearly 30 percent less.[12] A 2021 McKinsey study reported that while African Americans make up 12 percent of the U.S. population, they constituted only 7 percent of managers in corporate America and only 5 percent of senior managers.[13] At the current trajectory, it would take Black professionals nearly one hundred years to get to the proportionate representation of 12 percent in just the management ranks of corporate America.[14]

Dr. Martin Luther King spent the last years and days of his life fighting for economic justice as the next chapter in the civil rights movement. He recognized that power and participation in the economy were critical to social progress in America. Two weeks before he was assassinated, he gave a speech in Memphis, Tennessee, as part of his Poor People's Campaign for economic justice, highlighting the inextricable ties between civil rights and economic justice:

> With Selma and the voting rights bill one era of our struggle came to a close and a new era came into being. Now our struggle is for genuine equality, which means economic equality. For we know now that it isn't enough to integrate lunch counters. What does it profit a man to be able to eat at an integrated lunch counter if he doesn't earn enough money to buy a hamburger and a cup of coffee? What does it profit a man to be able to eat at the swankiest integrated restaurant when he doesn't earn enough money to take his wife out to dine? What does it profit one to have access to the hotels of our city and the motels of our highway when we don't earn enough money to take our family on

> a vacation? What does it profit one to be able to attend an integrated school when he doesn't earn enough money to buy his children school clothes?[15]

Businesses and business leaders are uniquely situated to help aid in what King called the struggle for genuine equality, because they control so many critical financial and economic levers. Through thoughtful corporate social activism, particularly when it complements public policy reforms, activists and capitalists can help undo some of the lasting legacies of America' original sin on matters of race.

THE PERNICIOUS PERSISTENCE OF GENDER INEQUALITY

Ever since Eve was blamed for Adam's taking a bite of the forbidden fruit and being banished from paradise in ancient religious texts, the female of our species has gotten a raw deal. Although women make up more than half of the world's population and make much of daily life possible with their underappreciated efforts, and despite progress in the developed nations, they are still largely disrespected, mistreated, and maligned.

The facts and figures are stark and startling. The gender gap between men and women is greatest along dimensions of economic and political power.[16] According to a 2018 World Economic Forum study, women are only at 59 percent parity in terms of economic power compared to their male counterparts, and 22 percent parity in terms of political power.[17] A 2020 World Bank Study indicated that women only have three-quarters of the legal rights of men around the world.[18] There are only six countries where there is no legal difference along gender lines.[19] Compared to men, women around the world also spend twice the amount of time doing unpaid work and shoulder the majority of childcare responsibilities.[20] In numerous countries around the world, there are laws limiting what daughters and wives can inherit, with no comparable restrictions for sons and husbands.[21] And these facts and figures are even worse for most women of color.

This is not a problem restricted to the third world or poor countries. This is a problem of the world, of all countries. The United States, the richest country in the world, continues to fall behind when it comes to gender equality. The United States is one of only eight countries in the world that does not offer government-sponsored paid maternity leave.[22] Women working full time make only 82 percent of what their male full-time counterparts do.[23] This pay gap exists in almost every profession, including the highest paying ones like medicine and finance.[24] A study from the American Association of University Women found that female doctors and surgeons suffer from a 29-percent gender pay gap, as they are paid only seventy-one cents for every dollar their male counterparts are paid.[25]

Because business enterprises are human enterprises, they often reflect and perpetuate the gender stereotypes and structural sexism that have been around for far too long because of a patriarchal society. This is evidenced in part by the recent #MeToo movement initiated by many brave women and men, which has precipitated a long-overdue examination of law, business, gender, dignity, and power throughout the business world and society. The recent iteration of the #MeToo movement has been an uncomfortable but necessary awakening for the business world and its executives. The current #MeToo movement was named by Tarana Burke, a social activist working with victims of sexual abuse, who first used the term "Me Too" in 2007.

In October 2017, the #MeToo hashtag went viral on social media when actress Alyssa Milano posted the following tweet "If you've been sexually harassed or assaulted write 'me too' as a reply to this tweet," which had the following caption: "Me too.

Suggested by a friend: 'If all the women who have been sexually harassed or assaulted wrote 'Me too' as a status, we might give people a sense of the magnitude of the problem.'" Following Milano's tweet, the #MeToo hashtag trended on Twitter, Facebook, Snapchat, and other leading social media platforms. On Facebook alone, it was shared in more than twelve million posts within the first twenty-four hours.[26] The effects of this movement continue to ripple throughout American business and society. Private or workplace sexual misconduct and other behavior by executives and colleagues that was previously tolerated or ignored is now deemed unacceptable and is subjected to greater scrutiny. Numerous high-profile corporate executives and celebrities have been removed or convicted of sexual misconduct as a result of this movement.

Yet despite the #MeToo movement, our government again failed to take any meaningful actions to combat this persistent problem. Instead, serious issues about gender equality devolved into fodder for cable news and social media.

In contrast, for many businesses the #MeToo movement was an inflection point to reexamine and reform longstanding corporate practices that harmed women in the workplace. Often working with activists, many companies established or bolstered programs to promote women within their firms and industries. Companies like Google pushed and funded programs for more female scientists and engineers. Other companies increased paid maternity leave. Still others offered more mentorship and support to help women advance across multiple industries. Netflix, for instance, commissioned a comprehensive diversity study that resulted in the company's investing $100 million to improve diversity in their films and shows, both in front of and behind the camera.

More significantly, many female entrepreneurs and celebrities used their influence and power to narrow the chasm of gender inequality through creative corporate acts of activism. Sallie Kraw-check, a former senior banking executive at Bank of America and Citigroup, formed Ellevest, a digital financial platform for female investors. Whitney Wolfe Herd, a tech entrepreneur, started Bumble, a billion-dollar dating app that empowered women to make the initial contact with potential dates. The Oscar-winning actress Reese Witherspoon started Hello Sunshine, a media company, to promote and produce the stories of women in film, television, and books. And for every one of these high-profile examples, there are thousands more women using business platforms to effectuate the change they want to see in the world.

These nontraditional efforts of corporate social activism on behalf of women are not just the right thing to do from a moral and social perspective; they are also the right thing to do from a business perspective. Companies with more gender diversity in their executive ranks tend to outperform their peers financially.[27] Other research suggests that more gender diversity makes firms more productive and creative.[28]

While activism in the commercial and economic space might seem very different from the traditional activism of marches and boycotts, it can be just as impactful, if not more so. Because businesses affect so much of what we see, hear, read, and do, having proper female representation and depictions can have a real and lasting impact, particularly for young women and girls, and society as a whole.

While there has been some progress on the challenges of gender equality, much more is needed, especially after the COVID-19 pandemic. The pandemic has disproportionately harmed women in terms of their careers, health, and safety. An Oxfam International study estimated that the pandemic cost women around the world "$800 billion in lost income in 2020, equivalent to more than the combined GDP of 98 countries."[29]

The pandemic has reversed so much of the progress that had occurred in the past few decades for women. More innovation and investment are needed on behalf of women.

Melinda French Gates called an investment in women "the most comprehensive, pervasive, high-leverage investment you can make in human beings."[30] In her inspiring book, *The Moment of Lift: How Empowering Women Changes the World*, she wrote of the importance of advancing women's rights for all of us:

> As women gain rights, families flourish, and so do societies. That connection is built on a simple truth: Whenever you include a group that's been excluded, you benefit everyone. And when you're working globally to include women and girls, who are half of every population, you're working to benefit all members of every community. Gender equity lifts everyone. Women's rights and society's health and wealth rise together. And so, through thoughtful corporate social activism, activists and capitalists can help lift up all of us and undo much of the wrongs that business interests have helped perpetuate in the past and present, while continuing to push for changes in public policy through a broken political process.[31]

THE FIGHT CONTINUES

The struggle for equality and justice persists in America. It often finds heart in the timely and timeless fights for equal protection and equal opportunity along the fault lines and intersections of race and gender. These fights take place in big cities and small towns, red states and blue states, courthouses and schoolhouses, on the streets, and online. And more and more, it is happening in the marketplace, with executive decisions, consumer choices, shareholder actions, and boardroom decisions. As such, capitalists and activists have joined forces in this long struggle over some of the endemic challenges that have plagued humanity and society.

Capitalists and activists can help to undo some of the harms that businesses have reinforced and perpetuated for too long to the detriment of too many. Activists can push capitalists to move more urgently and more empathetically. At the same time, capitalists can push activists to broaden and effectuate their real-world impact. Because so much of society is driven by economic activity, businesses can play a uniquely influential role in bringing about these changes.

Capitalists and activists should push businesses to help undo the persistent scourges of racism and sexism, not only because there is a strong moral case for it, but also because there is a strong business case for it. Numerous studies suggest that more diverse and compassionate businesses perform better as investments.[32] Furthermore, study after study shows that a more diverse workplace in terms of race, gender, and other intersectional demographic vectors is generally good for profits, productivity, and shareholder returns, to say nothing of its positive social impact.[33]

While every corporate initiative can seem too little, too slow, too late, and perhaps too disingenuous, these initiatives could also offer meaningful steps forward during a time when our politics seem so unwilling or unable to get near these sensitive fault lines and intersections of race and gender in a constructive way.

To be clear, no business initiative or program can serve as a substitute for landmark legislation like the civil rights acts of the

1960s, and businesses bear significant blame for some legacy caste systems that perpetuate systemic discrimination against minorities and women. That said, until there are civil rights breakthroughs in our politics, creative and swift actions from activists and capitalists can serve as powerful catalysts for change in public opinion and public life. As President Lyndon Johnson put it well in 1965 at Howard University:

> But freedom is not enough. You do not wipe away
> the scars of centuries by saying: Now you are free
> to go where you want, and do as you desire, and
> choose the leaders you please. You do not take a
> person who, for years, has been hobbled by chains
> and liberate him, bring him up to the starting line
> of a race and then say, "you are free to compete with
> all the others," and still justly believe that you have
> been completely fair. Thus it is not enough just to
> open the gates of opportunity. All our citizens must
> have the ability to walk through those gates. This is
> the next and the more profound stage of the battle
> for civil rights. We seek not just freedom but oppor-
> tunity. We seek not just legal equity but human
> ability, not just equality as a right and a theory but
> equality as a fact and equality as a result.[34]

Capitalists and activists—along with strong and sensible government leaders—should work together urgently and creatively to restructure broken systems, create meaningful opportunities, and empower everyone with the capabilities to flourish in a changing world.

CHAPTER 7

Better Activism, Better Business

AEROSMITH, THE AMERICAN ROCK BAND, was founded in Boston in 1970 with members Steven Tyler, Joe Perry, Tom Hamilton, Joey Kramer, and Ray Tabano, who would be replaced by Brad Whitford a year later. Their first decade was a successful one, with multiple multi-platinum albums and hits like "Dream On" and "Sweet Emotion," but at the end of their first decade, the band was beset with infighting, breakups, addiction, and other common curses of a rock-and-roll life.

As Aerosmith was losing its way at the start of the 1980s, down Interstate 95 from Boston, in New York City, Joseph Simmons, Daryl McDaniels, and Jason Mizell (aka Jam Master Jay) formed the hip-hop group Run-DMC. Its 1984 debut album, *Run-DMC*, achieved gold record status, selling over five hundred thousand units, the first hip-hop album to do so. Its follow-up album, *King of Rock*, went platinum, selling over one million units, again a first for a hip-hop group. Yet for all their success, talent, and innovative sounds, Run-DMC had not achieved mainstream success.

In 1986, the paths of Aerosmith and Run-DMC crossed when producer Rick Rubin urged Run-DMC to do a cover of the Aerosmith hit song "Walk This Way." The suggestion seemed far-fetched at the time because rock and hip-hop were widely considered distinct genres of music, each with its own audience and radio stations. Rock was considered mainstream; hip-hop was still an emerging, niche genre. Reluctantly, Run-DMC agreed to do the cover for their album, *Raising Hell*.

Aerosmith and Run-DMC came together on a Sunday afternoon in a New York City studio in 1986 and recorded a version of "Walk This Way" that broke down the divide between rock and hip-hop, infusing the record with the big guitar sound of hard rock and the beats and flow of rap. The song gave new life to Aerosmith and helped move Run-DMC and hip-hop into the mainstream. It introduced rock fans to hip-hop and hip-hop fans to rock. The song rocketed up into the top 10 of the Billboard Hot 100, with an iconic, groundbreaking music video on MTV.[1]

After "Walk This Way," Aerosmith began a multi-decade-long renaissance, became one of the greatest best-selling American bands of all time, and won numerous Grammy awards, while Run-DMC became one of the greatest and most influential hip-hop groups of all time. Both were inducted into the Rock and Roll Hall of Fame. "Walk This Way" is considered one of the greatest songs of all time by *Rolling Stone* and the Rock and Roll Hall of Fame.

Most importantly, "Walk This Way" tore down the decades-long arbitrary divide between rock and rap, between cultures and sounds that should never have been divided to begin with. Journalist Geoff Edgers, in his book, *Walk This Way: Run-DMC, Aerosmith, and the Song That Changed American Music Forever*, observed the significance of the track: "What none of them understood is that together, in a single Sunday afternoon in Manhattan, they would change not just music but society itself."[2]

Since then, any boundaries that had existed between rock and hip-hop have become blurred or erased. False notions of white music and Black urban music rightfully became a relic of a misguided past. Hip-hop beats became common in rock songs, and the powerful electric guitar rock sounds became part of hip-hop songs. It became common for hip-hop artists to make music with rockers. Kanye West collaborating with former Beatle Paul McCartney does not seem any less normal than Kanye West working with Jay-Z, or Taylor Swift working with Kendrick Lamar.

Just as the genre-breaking "Walk This Way" broke down the barriers between hip-hop and rock, making each of them distinctly and collectively better, the new business of social change reflected in contemporary corporate social activism can do the same for capitalism and activism. Contemporary corporate social activism offers the promise of simultaneously improving both activism and capitalism, of enhancing social value and shareholder value. Activists and capitalists can coexist and cooperate in a mutually beneficial symbiotic relationship. Activists and capitalists can recognize their differences and still work together to make one another better in service of a greater good.

By working with capitalists, activists can broaden and deepen the impact of their activism by leveraging the communication resources, political influence, and operational expertise of businesses for their causes. Rather than merely silo capitalists away or fight with businesses (who admittedly cause some of the problems that animate activism), activists can work with and learn from capitalists to help solve the social problems that confront them. Similarly, capitalists working with activists can establish broader corporate purposes and create new markets for their businesses.

BETTER ACTIVISM

The words you are reading in this book were initially typed using Microsoft Word, the dominant word processing program for decades, generating tens of billions of dollars in annual revenues as part of the productivity software suite known as Microsoft Office. If Word was a standalone company, it would be one of the most successful software companies of all time. Yet for Bill Gates, Microsoft Word and Microsoft Office would not even crack the top two of his lifetime achievements. Microsoft Windows, the dominant operating system for laptop and desktop computers, would be his most impactful corporate achievement. But more than controlling the operating system of nearly eight out of ten computers in the world on any given year, and more than being the default productivity software for people, Bill Gates's most impactful work is his advocacy and activism with the Gates Foundation on behalf of the poorest people in the world.

The Gates Foundation, established by Bill Gates and his former spouse, Melinda French Gates, is one of the largest foundations in the world, with a nearly $50 billion endowment.[3] It invests over $1 billion a year in the areas of global health and education.[4] Working with businesses, governments, and nongovernmental organizations, it has distributed hundreds of millions of life-saving vaccines in the developing world, and provided millions with better education and opportunities in the United States. By one estimate appearing in the *Guardian*, the Foundation's work has saved over a hundred million lives around the world.[5]

The Foundation has been so impactful not just because of the size of its endowment, but also because of the way they deployed it. The Gateses took the same business know-how and methods that brought Microsoft legendary business success and applied it to their Foundation's work in advocacy and activism. The goals are different, but their approaches in their Foundation's work are quite similar to their approaches with Microsoft—data-driven, iterative, efficient, and scalable.

Whereas the goal with Microsoft might have been 100-percent dominance with operating systems and productivity software, the goal of the foundation is total eradication of preventable diseases. Near the end of the Foundation's 2017 annual letter, Bill Gates wrote: "We want to end our letter with the most magical number we know. It's zero. This is the number we're striving toward every day at the foundation. Zero malaria. Zero TB. Zero HIV. Zero malnutrition. Zero preventable deaths. Zero difference between the health of a poor kid and every other kid."[6] Melinda French Gates noted, "Moving toward zero is perhaps the biggest difference between our philanthropy and a business. In the private sector, the goal is to stay in business. In our case, nothing would make us happier than going out of business because we've achieved our goals."[7]

To be sure, some of Microsoft's most aggressive business practices can be deemed anticompetitive, and some of Bill Gates's reported personal behavior during his time as an executive there and afterward was improper, inadvisable, and inexcusable. It is nevertheless hard to dismiss the innovation and impact that Microsoft and its thousands of employees have brought to modern life, and how some of the lessons developed at Microsoft have helped inform the innovation and success of the Gates Foundation and its impact on global health.

Inarguably, one of the most important lessons to be learned from the work of the Gates Foundation is that the best practices of the best businesses in the world, if borrowed and leveraged thoughtfully and empathetically by activists operating in the nonprofit space, can lead to more impactful activism. The rise of contemporary corporate social activism will provide ample opportunities for activists and capitalists to engage in this cross-cutting learning and leveraging. Generally speaking, nonprofit organizations engaged in activism and advocacy work have not always been very effective at sustaining their efforts and expanding their impact. Successful businesses grow and last over time because they are able to raise more capital, increase their market share, and attract talented individuals. Thus, by working with corporations who have expertise in communications, operations, and accountability, activists could improve the sustainability and impact of their efforts.

Communications

Activists can learn from and leverage the communications practices of businesses to create better, more impactful activism by breaking through some of the political obstacles and gridlock that frequently stand in the way of social change.

Corporate communications tools and platforms are some of the most powerful in the world. The same tools and methods that are used to convince millions of consumers to try a new product or service that they never knew they wanted can also be leveraged to convince people to see a social issue differently. The same tools and methods that are used to lobby politicians to lower taxes and cut regulations for businesses can also be used to lobby politicians to move on a social issue. Through the influential communication platforms of individual corporations or corporate trade associations, social issues can reach the masses and key decision-makers like never before, creating pressure to change laws and make new policies.

In 2015, with numerous states introducing so-called "religious freedom" and "bathroom" laws that discriminated against the LGBTQ community, Tim Cook, the CEO of Apple, wrote a powerful, widely read op-ed about the dangers of such discrimination and helped shape the larger conversation about those laws. Cook, writing on behalf of one of the most valuable companies in the world, helped activists frame the debate not just as a narrow one about LGBTQ rights but as a broader one about human dignity and an inviting business environment. Cook wrote:

> America's business community recognized a long time ago that discrimination, in all its forms, is bad for business. At Apple, we are in business to empower and enrich our customers' lives. We strive to do business in a way that is just and fair. That's why, on behalf of Apple, I'm standing up to oppose this new wave of legislation — wherever it emerges. I'm writing in the hopes that many more will join this movement. From North Carolina to Nevada, these bills under consideration truly will hurt jobs, growth and the economic vibrancy of parts of the country where a 21st-century economy was once welcomed with open arms.[8]

By partnering his powerful corporate communications platform with activists working on the issue, Cook was able to get through to politicians who might not have been receptive to that perspective had it come from an activist or from a vantage point rooted solely in LGBTQ rights. As a result of the efforts of activists and capitalists like Cook, numerous states ultimately vetoed or amended their "religious freedom" and "bathroom" laws for fear of losing business investments in their states.

By learning, leveraging, and working smartly with corporations and their communications assets, activists can help ensure that well-known social issues benefit from wider understanding and thoughtful discussion, and that less-well-known issues benefit from reaching larger, key audiences.

Operations

Through contemporary corporate social activism, activists can learn from and leverage the best practices of business operations to create more effective and efficient activism. The tools and principles that allow successful businesses to serve their customers in a complicated world can also be used to aid activists in their causes, serving as a kind of force multiplier and accelerant to their traditional efforts.

Corporations, particularly large global ones, can help activists become more effective by working through or bypassing complex domestic and international barriers in ways that government officials simply cannot, due to the constraints of contemporary politics and international relations. Global corporations can serve as powerful private channels to address large problems in ways that are difficult for governments and activists alone, given domestic and international political concerns. Where government personnel and activists may have a hard time operating alone in foreign countries without raising the suspicions and ire of foreign authorities, businesses can do so more readily. Western Union, for example, regularly assists numerous nongovernmental and advocacy organizations with their payment systems to transfer funds to remote parts of the world to aid those in need, without having to negotiate with governments that are frequently unfriendly to such organizations and outside funding.[9]

Similarly, the logistical expertise of businesses can be leveraged to help activists deepen the impact of their efforts by solving complex coordination and organizational challenges. For instance, Coca-Cola's expertise in storing and distributing beverages globally can be incredibly beneficial to organizations working to distribute food, medicine, and other supplies to remote parts of the world. After all, almost every village you go to in the world, however remote, has Coca-Cola. In fact, the Gates Foundation partnered with Coca-Cola in 2010 to use its "logistic, supply chain and marketing expertise" to distribute critical medicine to areas in Africa, which was previously a particularly frustrating problem for many nonprofit organizations and local governments.[10]

Accountability

Activists working with businesses can learn and leverage the best business practices of accountability to help expand and deepen their impact using data-driven approaches that are the hallmark of the best businesses. Because good businesses are accountable to efficiently maximizing returns for their shareholders in a sustainable fashion, they are likely to bring that same data-driven, market-oriented mind-set to their social activism efforts. As such, contemporary corporate social activism can push activists working in the nonprofit space to embrace the best accountability and data-driven processes of businesses in their operations.

Activist organizations thus take on more of a business-oriented, investment posture and less of a charity-oriented, nonprofit posture. This new approach has been characterized by some as "philanthrocapitalism," "social entrepreneurship," or "creative capitalism."[11] Former dean of Harvard Law School Martha Minow cited one in her book *Partners, Not Rivals: Privatization and the Public Good*: "Social entrepreneurship is a new buzzword to characterize efforts by philanthropists to bring market-style ideas or business accountability methods to philanthropic investment."[12] But at its core, this approach is simply a more efficient and more accountable form of activism.

Contemporary corporate social activism pushes good activists to think a little more like good capitalists, to consider how better to use their limited capital to achieve the greatest impact from, and return for their efforts. Social activism thus becomes less akin to charity or volunteerism and more akin to social investment or venture philanthropy. With more emphasis on thoughtful capital management, activism can take on more of an investment mind-set—an approach that may be more effective than traditional practices, wherein businesses donate funds with no active engagement as to how those funds are operationalized or managed by others.

This move toward greater businesslike accountability may be not only desirable by activists and advocacy organizations, but also necessary, given the fact that many preeminent philanthropists that are tackling large social issues today are current and former corporate technology titans, like Mark Zuckerberg of Facebook and Marc Benioff of Salesforce. Capitalists like Zuckerberg and Benioff consider their contributions and efforts less as gifts and more as investments in society. They carefully track investments, measure results, and study how best to generate better returns, so as to attract even more capital to tackle big social problems in creative ways.

In fact, many contemporary philanthropic organizations are set up as flexible investment vehicles aimed at tackling large social issues through both traditional philanthropic grants and equity investments. The Chan Zuckerberg Initiative—created by Mark Zuckerberg and his wife, Dr. Priscilla Chan—is organized as a limited liability company, with billions of dollars in assets, and is designed, in part, to make investments in research and businesses that help cure the world's diseases. Similarly, the

Emerson Collective, a limited liability organization founded by Steve Jobs's widow, Laurene Powell Jobs, uses similar business-oriented accountability approaches in pursuit of their activism.[13] The Collective has investments in media outlets like the *Atlantic* and *Axios* to help ensure good journalism on issues like education, immigration, and climate change.

Ultimately, by learning from and leveraging the communications, operations, and accountability of the best businesses, activists can create more meaningful, sustainable, and expansive impacts for their causes.

BETTER BUSINESS

It was one of the greatest cities in the world. An unparalleled hub of technology, industry, sports, and culture. It was a city where blue-collar workers and white-collar executives both prospered. It was a city that helped to define music as we know it. It had growth, grit, and glamour. It was Detroit, Michigan—the birthplace of the modern automobile, the home of Motown Records, and a citadel of organized labor. For much of the first half of the twentieth century, Detroit was one of the most celebrated cities in the world.

Then the tides of history turned. A cold wind blew in, creating a multi-decade-long lake effect that chilled the once glorious city's promise and growth. Detroit's boom and glory began to decline in the 1950s as its population escaped to the suburbs. The 1960s brought about unrest and race riots that led to thousands of arrests and thousands of buildings destroyed. The 1970s saw further decline and municipal corruption that induced more flight from the city. The decades that followed saw an acceleration of the fall of this great city through forces beyond its control, like globalization, as well as forces more within its control, like government corruption. One of America's wealthiest and most shining cities became one of its poorest and grayest within the span of a few decades.

At the start of the twenty-first century, Detroit was a city in crisis. In 2008, Detroit mayor Kwame Kilpatrick was convicted of various felonies for misconduct and abuse of power and was forced to resign. Five years later, in 2013, he was convicted on an additional twenty-four counts of federal crimes in connection with municipal corruption and sentenced to nearly thirty years in prison. In July 2013, the city filed for bankruptcy, the largest bankruptcy ever of an American city.

Detroit, throughout its struggles, nevertheless has remained in the American consciousness. Too often, politicians used the city as a backdrop for photo ops as they peddled false hope and empty promises in an election year in exchange for votes.

For others, Detroit remained in their minds because Detroit was more than one Rust Belt city fallen on hard times. It was representative of all the American cities that had fallen on hard times and trying to find their way back. The journalist Charlie LeDuff eloquently opined in *Detroit: An American Autopsy*: "But I believe that Detroit is America's city. It was the vanguard of our way up, just as it is the vanguard of our way down. And one hopes the vanguard of our way up again. Detroit is Pax Americana."[14]

Yet, throughout the tumultuous fall of this great American city, many of its resilient citizens remained and fought to make it better.

In 2014, JPMorgan Chase, one of the largest financial institutions in the world, decided to make an audacious multi-million-dollar, multiyear commitment to revitalize Detroit. The bank partnered with local activist organizations, business executives, and government leaders to better execute their commitment. In the first five years of its commitment, JPMorgan invested over $100 million in the city through an assortment of programs, and then expanded its commitment to reach $200 million by the year 2022.[15]

The commitment, as outlined and executed by CEO Jamie Dimon, was not just to lend money to Detroit and its local businesses; rather, JPMorgan Chase was going to invest its institutional time, resources, and expertise in connection with its capital. It used its institutional data and research capabilities to help establish skills training programs, jump-start financial education initiatives, and offer risk assessment tools for developers and investors to attract more people and jobs to Detroit. As a result of its efforts, thousands of small businesses received additional capital, tens of thousands of Detroiters obtained skills training and financial education, thousands of new jobs were created, and thousands of new affordable housing units were built.[16]

Because JPMorgan Chase worked with local leaders in activism, business, and government, they were able to better identify the city's needs and deploy their expertise in a more targeted, effective fashion. For example, a local community financial institution, InvestDetroit, working in small business and real estate development, needed help gathering data to identify which neighborhoods were most suitable for various investments and projects.[17] In response, JPMorgan Chase brought in a team of its data scientists to create a user-friendly data system to help local banks, entrepreneurs, and government officials identify and quantify neighborhood health and neighborhood needs.[18] The database they created through their work with local advocacy groups allows local businesses and entrepreneurs to forecast whether a restaurant, grocery, coffee shop, or other type of business is likely to succeed in any given block of Detroit. This type of expertise was previously available only to JPMorgan Chase and its best clients (read: highest-fee-paying clients), and now it is available to small businesses, advocacy organizations, and entrepreneurs in Detroit.

JPMorgan Chase's commitment to Detroit was also a commitment to do something different in its philanthropic efforts. While the bank has historically given hundreds of millions of dollars away annually to local communities and worthy causes, the commitment to Detroit represented a concerted, sustained effort to focus its corporate social and philanthropic efforts on economic revitalization and financial counseling, two areas where the bank has superior competencies.

This new approach represented a shift in both the focus and the mode of corporate social activism. JPMorgan Chase's commitment in Detroit was not just a one-off financial donation or a flashy passing effort done in a few days; rather, it was a sustained engagement of financial capital, social capital, and intellectual capital. It was an investment in Detroit with expectations of returns for the city and the bank. As Detroit revitalized, its citizens and businesses would need banking services, and JPMorgan Chase wanted to be the bank of Detroit. CEO Jamie Dimon remarked about the bank's position in the city: "Chase is the home bank," with 65 percent market share in consumer banking in the city with a growing position.[19] The work of JPMorgan Chase along with local activists, businesses, and elected officials created more opportunities and positive outcomes for the company and the city.

In the first six years of JPMorgan Chase's commitment to Detroit, the city saw increases in real per capita income and "gross city product," based on data collected by the Federal Reserve Bank of Chicago.[20] Given its successes in Detroit,

JPMorgan Chase started rolling out similar initiatives in other American cities that have fallen on tough times.

The JPMorgan Chase commitment to Detroit highlights how corporate social activism, when thoughtfully executed, can create sustainable benefits not just for causes and communities, but also for the companies themselves. Just as corporate social activism can make activism better, it can also make businesses better by expanding marketplaces and attracting better investors.

New and Better Markets

Contemporary social activism that thoughtfully partners capitalists with activists to solve social problems can not only help activists and their causes but also create new and better markets for businesses. By engaging in meaningful corporate social activism, firms can distinguish their brand value and expand the markets for their goods and services to customers that they previously did not attract. Moreover, these engagements could also create opportunities for businesses to innovate and help their bottom lines.

As an example, Levi Strauss, the over-150-year-old company known throughout the world for its denim jeans, worked with sustainable apparel activists to create trademarked "WaterLess" jeans that use significantly less water in the production process to help conserve water.[21] These efforts not only aided the cause of sustainable apparel activists but also created a new line of eco-friendly clothes for Levi's and helped the company innovate its production processes.

Similarly, Walmart's partnership with the Environmental Defense Fund to tackle environmental issues has helped the company launch new sources of revenue via environmentally friendly products and cost savings through smarter energy practices, while simultaneously furthering the objectives of environmentalists.[22]

Now, entire businesses are being launched with social activism built into the company's DNA. For instance, the eyewear company Warby Parker began by trying to solve the problem of expensive glasses in a marketplace dominated by Luxottica. To distinguish itself from the established leader in its space for selling what is ostensibly a commodity, Warby Parker decided right from the start that whenever a customer bought a pair of its affordable glasses it would donate a pair for someone less fortunate in need of eyewear through its partnership with the vision advocacy group VisionSpring.[23] In the company's first decade, it has given hundreds of thousands of pairs of glasses away to people with vision impairment in over fifty countries, including the United States.

New Investors

Smart corporate social activism can benefit companies by attracting new investors, as new sources of capital.

In fact, one of the fastest-growing areas in investment management in recent years has been *impact or social investing*. The term refers to investments that seek positive financial returns while aiming to make a positive social impact, particularly on environmental, social, and governance (ESG) challenges. In a 2019 study of institutional investors, 84 percent of the institutional investors surveyed believed that corporations should have a commitment to multiple stakeholders impacted by their companies.[24] Today, all major mutual fund companies and money managers—such as Vanguard, BlackRock, and Fidelity—offer numerous social or impact investment options.

These investment managers are not seeking impact or social investment purely for doing social good. They also want to do well financially for their clients and themselves. And in many instances, doing good for society need not come at the cost of negative or lower financial returns. Recent research suggests that socially active and responsible businesses that focus on multiple stakeholders generate stronger returns for their shareholders and have greater brand value in the marketplace.[25]

Furthermore, many companies have publicly pledged to promote ESG factors in their business and disclosure practices, to better attract the capital of more socially conscious, long-term investors, among an ever-expanding and diversifying population of investors. One of the largest and fastest-growing investor populations is the millennial generation. According to multiple studies and surveys, this large and growing category of investors cares deeply about the social standing and activism of the companies that they shop with or invest in.[26] According to research from the investment bank UBS, "Almost two-thirds of American millennials are highly interested—not just simply interested—in sustainable investing."[27] This view of impact investments extends beyond issues concerning environment and sustainability to social issues like racial justice and inclusion. As such, if businesses want to attract and retain this growing investor class, and investments in general, it may be not only desirable but also necessary for them to be socially active and socially engaged in the world.

By the end of 2020, ESG investments accounted for one-third of all invested assets under management, or around $17 trillion.[28] It would not be surprising, given current trends in investments and business practices, if in the future nearly all investments became some variation of ESG investments. An ESG investment would simply be an investment.

MUTUAL BENEFITS OF CORPORATE SOCIAL ACTIVISM

The rise of corporate social activism in contemporary society presents an incredible opportunity that could be mutually beneficial to activists and capitalists. More specifically, by working with businesses, activists could gain wider reach, deeper impact, and improved operations. At the same time, by working with activists, capitalists could enhance their value and create new and better markets, and attract more investors to their businesses. This does not mean corporate social activism will always work in a mutually beneficial way, nor does it mean that benefits for activists and capitalists will always be equally or fairly distributed. Rather, it means that corporate social activism represents a new path that can symbiotically join the forces of capitalism with the forces of activism toward meaningful profit and progress. It represents a pragmatic, underappreciated path forward toward creating better activism, better capitalism, and a better society.

CHAPTER 8

The Perils of Corporate Social Activism

I N AUGUST 2019, THERE WERE LINES around America. People lined up for hours. They were lining up for a chicken sandwich: Popeyes' new spicy chicken sandwich. The sandwich was launched via a tweet that quickly went viral. Popeyes outlets saw long, boisterous lines around the country after the tweet, a common scene outside of limited-edition sneaker releases at Foot Locker, but never before for a fast-food chain offering. A man in Maryland was even killed during an argument while waiting in line for the sandwich.[1] The Popeyes chicken sandwich sold out nationwide a few weeks later and was unavailable for several months.

Popeyes' chicken sandwich offering kicked off what trade publication *Food Business News* called "the chicken sandwich wars," as companies like McDonald's, Wendy's, and KFC raced to dominate this market that could be worth billions of dollars in annual sales.[2]

The dominant company in the chicken sandwich market is Chick-fil-A, a privately held, family-owned chain that touts itself as the "Home of the Original Sandwich." The company was founded by S. Truett Cathy, a deeply devout conservative Southern Baptist Christian. Cathy infused the company with his religious beliefs. Chick-fil-A's corporate purpose is "to glorify God by being a faithful steward of all that is entrusted to us and to have a positive influence on all who come into contact with Chick-fil-A."[3] The company's restaurants are all closed on Sundays to allow their employees to rest and go to church. Chick-fil-A also has robust programs to help and give back to local communities through its foundation and restaurants.[4]

In the summer of 2012, Chick-fil-A garnered national attention for something quite different from its chicken sandwiches or ads starring cows urging people to "Eat Mor Chikin." Dan Cathy, the founder's son and then president and chief operating officer of the company, spoke out against same-sex marriage on a radio show, saying in part, "I think we are inviting God's judgment on our nation when we shake our fist at Him and say, 'We know better than you as to what constitutes a marriage.' I pray God's mercy on our generation that has such a prideful, arrogant attitude to think that we have the audacity to define what marriage is about."[5] The statement, coupled with the company's longstanding donations to anti-LGBTQ organizations, angered many people and drew strong condemnations from LGBTQ activists and supporters. Customers boycotted Chick-fil-A outlets. Universities closed campus restaurants. Mayors of cities like Boston and Chicago denounced the company and tried to bar it from their cities.

Just as Chick-fil-A drew rebuke from LGBTQ activists and supporters, they also drew significant support from those who shared the Cathy family's traditional views on marriage. The boycott of Chick-fil-A was met with a counter-boycott initiated by former Arkansas governor Mike Huckabee. People who supported traditional marriage between a man and woman saw Chick-fil-A not just as a restaurant but as a vehicle for expressing their political position on a deeply personal issue. For a brief time, politicians used the restaurant's chicken sandwiches not just as a delivery vehicle for fried chicken, but also as a political prop.

A fast-food chicken sandwich became peppered with powerful political ramifications.

Over time, given all the controversy and unwanted attention, Chick-fil-A ceased corporate donations to anti-LGBTQ organizations and explicitly removed itself from any policy debates on same-sex marriage. Through a press release it stated:

> Going forward, our intent is to leave the policy debate over same-sex marriage to the government and political arena. Our mission is simple: to serve great food, provide genuine hospitality and have a positive influence on all who come in contact with Chick-fil-A.[6]

In the years that followed, Chick-fil-A continued to grow successfully across the country, with some of its largest and most prominent restaurants in the heart of New York City, one of the most liberal and LGBTQ-friendly cities in America.

The Chick-fil-A controversy highlights some of the potential drawbacks and pitfalls that can arise from contemporary corporate social activism. While the benefits and promise of contemporary corporate social activism are real and many, so are its costs and perils. In particular, contemporary corporate social activism can lead to political polarization in the marketplace, marginalization of important social issues, diminishment of democratic values, and corporate whitewashing.

RED BUSINESSES AND BLUE BUSINESSES

The rise of contemporary corporate social activism could further politicize the marketplace and polarize an already divided society. The new corporate social activism is a nonpartisan phenomenon. It can affect causes on both the political left and right, with many corporations taking crosscutting positions along the political spectrum. For instance, some corporations may support progressive positions on issues relating to LGBTQ rights and racial diversity but oppose progressive positions on issues relating to income inequality, corporate taxes, and health care access. The engagement and injection of politics into commerce and business could cause serious harm for companies and society, as politicians, policymakers, and consumers react to corporate social activism, and the polarization and division of the political arena bleeds into the commercial arena.

As corporations become more engaged in social issues, they will draw greater scrutiny from policymakers and politicians as they decry what they deem to be "woke" businesses and executives. Politicians could target businesses that take social positions adverse to their political interests for investigations, regulation, and other punitive actions, like cancelation of tax subsidies and government contracts or divestments from state pension funds. For instance, Georgia eliminated a $50 million tax break for Delta Airlines in 2018 as retaliation for the company's decision to cancel discounts to NRA members after the Parkland school shooting.[7]

Contemporary corporate social activism could also lead to greater polarization in the marketplace, as consumer choices become tinged with social and political judgment. Businesses wading into contentious social issues could lead to further consumer scrutiny and fragment the marketplace. Social media has magnified this scrutiny exponentially, and there are even activist organizations dedicated to examining and influencing business spending on advertising and other matters. This new attention frequently takes on a political dimension during an era of hyperpartisanship. Thus, just as politics has divided the country into red and blue, contemporary corporate social activism could fragment the marketplace into red businesses and blue businesses.

This politicization of the marketplace would alienate many customers and investors—and energize activists with opposing views all to the detriment of businesses. During the Trump administration, a number of businesses received unwanted attention for simply either serving or refusing to serve officials of the administration.

In 2018, a small family-owned Houston restaurant, El Tiempo Cantina, received backlash when it posted on Facebook that it was "an honor" to serve then U.S. attorney general Jeff Sessions.[8] Many Houstonians saw the post as an endorsement of Sessions's immigration policies. The restaurant owners then posted the following statement:

> El Tiempo does not in anyway [sic] support the
> practice of separating children from parents or any
> other practices of the government relative to immi
> gration. The posting of a photograph of the Attorney
> General at one of our restaurants does not represent
> us supporting his positions. . . . The man came to
> dinner and he was served without us even thinking
> about the political situations. . . . The only thing on
> our minds was serving great food and giving great

customer service. It was posted without review or
approval by ownership and this has lead [*sic*] to
everyone jumping to conclusions that somehow
we are involved in this political matter. We don't
approve of anyone separating parents and children.[9]

Not surprisingly, the statement then drew even more backlash and criticism from supporters of the Trump administration's immigration policy. Throughout this ordeal, this small business endured multiple protests, boycotts, counterprotests, and even death threats.

This politicization of the marketplace can be perilous for businesses, and angst-inducing for everyone. While consumers can use their consumption choices as an expression of their social or political views, not every choice is tinged with social or political judgment, nor should it be viewed as such.

Consumption choices can be complex or simple and do not always reflect one's views on any issue. A customer who shops at Walmart because of its low prices does not necessarily endorse its labor practices. A student who buys an iPhone because of its camera does not have to discount Apple's troubling use of foreign manufacturers. A small business owner that banks with their local Wells Fargo branch because of convenience does not have to agree with all of the company's mortgage practices or overdraft fees. A restaurateur that advertises on Google and Facebook does not necessarily endorse their privacy practices. A union autoworker with an Amazon Prime subscription does not necessarily subscribe to the company's anti-union positions. A woman who gases her car at an Exxon station is not making a social statement about climate policy any more than a man who buys a certain brand of hummus is making a statement about the conflicts in the Middle East. Yes, consumption decisions can have social and political ramifications. But sometimes they are just choices of convenience, cost, or taste.

Contemporary corporate social activism, if engaged in unwisely and without empathy, could lead to perilous polarization in the marketplace that causes people to view businesses and business transactions through a purely political lens. This can actually make social change through corporate activism more difficult in the same way that polarization has wrecked our political processes.

MARGINALIZATION OF IMPORTANT ISSUES

The rise of corporate social activism could marginalize important but discrete issues, as an elite managerial business class ascends to set much of the sociopolitical agenda. If, through corporate social activism, businesses become the outsized source of support or the primary agenda-setter for social change, there is a legitimate fear that some issues—particularly smaller, discrete issues—could become marginalized, as a corporate elite picks and prioritizes sociopolitical causes.

There is a legitimate concern that certain issues will simply be overlooked or marginalized by a largely homogenous group of powerful senior corporate executives, given the lack of diversity in the boardrooms of corporate America. A 2018 study by Deloitte reported that 84 percent of Fortune 500 board members are white, and just 16 percent of board members are minorities.[10] Additionally, the study revealed that nearly 78 percent of corporate directors are male.[11] Consequently, regardless of how woke or empathetic they may be, it may nevertheless be difficult for millionaire or billionaire corporate executives to understand the real concerns of their working-class employees, customers, shareholders, or citizens that make up the bulk of society.

Business elites will likely prefer to work on issues where they can garner the most positive publicity for their company or on pet causes of senior executives in addition to doing good, thus causing certain social issues to be orphaned or marginalized. Executives, fearful of boycotts and backlash from the public, may understandably shy away from speaking out on issues that could alienate or offend key customers, suppliers, or markets, in favor of issues that have broader appeal. For instance, a company that receives a significant amount of revenue from one country may be reticent to engage in social activism dedicated to improving human rights conditions in that country, for fear of offending its government. Similarly, companies with a large base of progressive millennial consumers will be more inclined to work on prominent progressive issues, like environmental sustainability, gender equality, workforce diversity, or LGBTQ rights. Conversely, activists for issues that are not aligned with those of powerful progressive corporate interests—issues like religious and conservative social causes—probably feel like their voices and views are already marginalized in contemporary society.

Moreover, capitalists are in the business of pursuing profit, so when given a choice, they may shy away from engaging in social issues that hurt their bottom lines in the near term. Many businesses are unlikely to willingly get deeply and seriously involved in sustained activism that would result in higher corporate taxes, more regulations, or additional labor costs, because these issues could directly impact the operations of their enterprises. Instead, it may be more convenient to engage in social issues that have a more tangential impact on their business but nevertheless a meaningful impact on society. This mind-set could ultimately marginalize important issues from the sociopolitical agenda.

THE RISE OF MARKET VALUES

The rise of contemporary corporate social activism could lead to a rise of market values and a corrosion of core democratic and moral values while corporate values continue to evolve. As more social activism efforts shift to private businesses, and thus people look to businesses to solve society's problems, this could weaken our democratic institutions and processes, along with the public's faith in them. This potentially corrosive effect could harm both corporations and social activists, as corporations—which are designed for profit generation—are not democracies and do not necessarily reflect the choices and values of a democratic society.

As businesses become more engaged in contentious social issues through corporate social activism, the market values of businesses could distort and subvert the democratic and moral values of society. People disillusioned with dysfunctional government could find greater affinity for private market solutions and disengage from political processes. As the renowned Harvard University political philosopher Michael Sandel observed in his book *What Money Can't Buy: The Moral Limits of Markets*: "Altruism, generosity, solidarity and civic spirit are not like commodities that are depleted with use. They are more like muscles that develop and grow stronger with exercise. One of the defects of a market-driven society is that it lets these virtues languish. To renew our public life we need to exercise them more strenuously."[12]

With the rise of corporate social activism, people can lose faith in our democratic institutions and pivot toward businesses. They may expect government to be operated more like a business, using purely market-driven values to solve society's ills. This can be highly problematic, because while corporations exist for the primary pursuit of profit, there are other civic priorities and public pursuits that cannot be measured by profit. There are civic priorities and public pursuits that are simply too big and complicated for private businesses to address using market tools and values alone.

Common corporate aims of efficiency and profit may contradict the values of justice and equal protection that activists have fought long and hard for and paid for dearly with blood and lives. Caring for the sick, weak, and poor may be unprofitable and unglamorous, but these are nevertheless worthy pursuits of a compassionate, democratic society. Similarly, social initiatives like disaster relief, public safety, disease control, and access to education should never be driven entirely by revenue or profits.

Government simply cannot be run like a for-profit business. Former New Orleans mayor Mitch Landrieu observed: "Government is not a business and the idea of 'running government as a business,' while a great line for TV spots, does not work as a political reality. Businesses function to earn a profit; cities are governed to deliver public services. . . . You can employ 'best practices' to weed out rot or improve delivery of services; but you don't run a police department or any public works department to make a profit."[13]

While many corporations have become more socially responsible, corporations, as well as the laws and norms that govern them, still focus keenly on profits for shareholders. This focus will naturally constrain and contradict some of their most noble social impulses. This focus, if misdirected by amoral or immoral management, can lead businesses to pursue profit at great harm to society. For instance, a pharmaceutical company focused largely on short-term profits can drastically reduce research and development and aggressively market highly profitable but addictive opioids, to the detriment of society. The opioid epidemic that has devastated many families and communities in the United States in recent years can be traced in part to poor, callous corporate decisions guided by profit-seeking at all costs.

A narrow, zealous focus on profits can also lead corporations to take actions and engage with parties that activists driven by different values would eschew. Not surprisingly, businesses guided by the amoral pursuit of profit regularly and readily work with autocratic and tyrannical regimes in ways that activists and others guided by higher values would not. Joel Bakan, in his book *The Corporation: The Pathological Pursuit of Profit and Power*, critically observed that "corporations have no capacity to value political systems, fascist or democratic, for reasons of principle or ideology."[14] This, of course, is not a new development. As an extreme historical example, during World War II, IBM worked with Nazi Germany in connection with the Holocaust, as chronicled in Edwin Black's book *IBM and the Holocaust: The Strategic Alliance Between Nazi Germany and America's Most Powerful Corporation*.[15] In the decades since this dark period in its corporate history, IBM has made numerous strides to be a more socially conscious corporate citizen of the world.

Understandably, some have argued that an engaged civil society of citizen-investors can mitigate some corporate vices, particularly the most extreme ones, through what the U.S. Supreme Court called "the procedures of corporate democracy."[16] That said, it is important to note that corporate democracy does not operate like political democracy. In contrast to political democracies, which adhere to the "one person, one vote" principle, corporate democracies adhere to a "one share, one vote" principle. Whereas the ideals of political democracy strive to treat all voters equally, the corporate democracy explicitly benefits large shareholders. As such, large, active shareholders with short-term agendas that are inconsistent with either a corporation's values or a community's core social values may dictate the actions in a corporate democracy.

Furthermore, just as political voting and corporate voting are fundamentally different, shareholders of a corporation are fundamentally different from citizens of a society. Shareholders frequently choose to be part of a corporation by buying into a company; in contrast, many citizens do not choose to be part of a country. Shareholders in a corporate democracy that disagree with the corporation's actions and values can readily sell their shares; citizens of a democratic society cannot readily leave their communities without incurring significant costs.

Given these differences, there is a real risk that corporate social activism, if engaged in thoughtlessly, can lead to the undermining of democratic values and civic institutions by market values and business institutions.

THE DANGER OF CORPORATE WHITEWASHING

The rise of contemporary corporate social activism presents a dangerously convenient and powerful vehicle for businesses to suppress activism against their own misdeeds. Such whitewashing can make it harder for activists and the government to hold businesses accountable for their misconduct and its negative social effects.

By working with activists on certain important social issues, companies can—whether wittingly or unwittingly—divert attention away from some of their more problematic business practices and enhance their public image in the eyes of society. A large energy company, for instance, can curry favor with the public by engaging with social activism on the important issues of racial justice and gender inclusion, thereby deflecting from themselves public scrutiny on issues involving the environment and climate change. Similarly, companies and executives can use their powerful communications machinery to influence policy-makers and regulators through activism on their own issues to divert attention from problems of their own making.

More nefariously, companies and executives can covertly initiate so-called "astroturf activism" to generate the misper-ception that there is strong, genuine grassroots support of cer-tain issues that benefits their bottom line.[17] This type of faux activism usually takes the form of corporate funds supporting an innocuous-sounding front entity masquerading as a grass-roots people's campaign. A classic case of astroturf activism was the National Smoker's Alliance, a purported grassroots organization of citizens who cared about the rights of Amer-ican cigarette smokers. The Alliance was formed in 1993 and used by pro-tobacco policymakers as a sign of popular opposi-tion to antismoking legislative proposals. It was later revealed that the Alliance was actually funded and constituted with the aid of large tobacco companies, like Philip Morris, to white-wash their cancer-inducing, profit-maximizing objectives with the veneer of populist support.

Part of the danger of corporate social activism is that by using the gloss of generous, highly efficient private solutions it can blind us to some of the persistent systemic problems caused by business interests and business elites. The keen and provocative writer Anand Giridharadas, in his insightful jeremiad of a book, *Winners Take All: The Elite Charade of Changing the World*, inci-sively diagnosed this danger:

> In an age defined by a chasm between those
> who have power and those who don't, elites have
> spread the idea that people must be helped, but
> only in market-friendly ways that do not upset

fundamental power equations. The society should
be changed in ways that do not change the underlying economic system that has allowed the winners
to win and fostered many of the problems they
seek to solve. The broad fidelity to this law helps
make sense of what we observe all around: the
powerful fighting to "change the world" in ways
that essentially keep it the same, and "giving back"
in ways that sustain an indefensible distribution of
influence, resources, and tools.[18]

Whether the results of business elites engaging in social
activism are as wholly devastating and irredeemable as Giridharadas and others have alleged is subject to legitimate debate.
While one could take a different, more optimistic view—that
economic institutions and systems are capable of evolving and
changing—one should nevertheless be clear-eyed about the
potential risks to activism, democratic institutions, and society
writ large that are posed by businesses and business elites as
they engage in social activism.

PITFALLS AND PROGRESS

The rise of corporate social activism in contemporary society presents incredible opportunities for social change, but this
ascendency also poses perilous pitfalls for businesses, activists, and society. Specifically, this rise could polarize an already
fragmented marketplace, marginalize important social issues,
corrode core democratic values, and whitewash corporate misdeeds. While capitalists and activists can and should learn and
benefit from working with one another, there are real risks and
drawbacks in this partnership, if engaged in thoughtlessly. These

risks and drawbacks can understandably cause one to recoil from working with businesses and business elites on social issues altogether. But with such a blanket withdrawal one would both deny the reality that corporate social activism is already happening and lose out on the potential good that can come from working with good people in business. Instead of refusing to engage in corporate social activism altogether, we must acknowledge its risks and manage them thoughtfully, honestly, and critically, so that society may realize its promise while sidestepping its perils.

CHAPTER 9

The New Business of Change

HE LOVED ICE CREAM, BUT HE COULD NEVER TASTE or smell it, because he suffered from a rare condition called anosmia.[1]

He and his childhood buddy would take a correspondence course on ice cream making and open a small ice cream shop in an abandoned gas station in Burlington, Vermont, in the spring of 1978. Because he could not really taste or smell the product he was selling, he decided to add chunks to it so that customers could gain another sensory experience with ice cream.

He was Ben Cohen. His childhood buddy was Jerry Greenfield. Their company was Ben & Jerry's. The company would end up making a huge difference in business and society, and along the way make a ton of ice cream with flavors like Half Baked, Cherry Garcia, Chocolate Fudge Brownie, Phish Food, and Americone Dream.

What made Ben & Jerry's special as a business was that its founders encoded a social mission into the company's DNA from the beginning. The company has a three-part economic, product, and social mission of linked prosperity. According to the company, "Our Economic Mission asks us to manage our Company for sustainable financial growth. Our Product Mission drives us to make fantastic ice cream—for its own sake. Our Social Mission compels us to use our Company in innovative ways to make the world a better place."[2]

To be sure, Ben & Jerry's took each part of its mission quite seriously. It grew sensibly by focusing not just on shareholders and profits but also on a collection of stakeholders that could help the company's bottom line over the long run. The company also continued innovating in its products, with new flavors and ingredients like cookie dough, fudge chunks, walnuts, waffle cones, and marshmallows. And it continued to focus on bettering the local community and the world at large. It used fair trade ingredients and organic milk from family dairy farms to make its products. It took public positions on social issues like systemic racism, same-sex marriage, fair trade, and climate change.

Over time, the company, with its three-pronged mission, grew from a little ice cream shop in Burlington to a regional, then a national company. In 1984 it became a publicly traded company listed on the NASDAQ. Yet, the company continued to stay true to its socially active roots. It set up a foundation to help local communities and global causes, and the company donated 7.5 percent of its profits annually to the foundation. In addition to its growing impact, it was growing in sales and profits.

In 2000, during a period when the stock languished, Ben & Jerry's received multiple takeover and merger overtures. After serious consideration, the owners ultimately, albeit reluctantly, decided to sell the company to the giant European conglomerate

Unilever for about $326 million. Unilever is one of the largest companies in the world, with some of the most well-known consumer brands, like Dove, Breyer's, Hellmann's, Lipton, and Vaseline. Through extended negotiations, Ben & Jerry's exacted several measures from Unilever to help protect its culture and social mission. Unilever gave Ben & Jerry's more autonomy than it gave any of its other subsidiaries. Unilever continued to fund the company's foundation generously, at 7.5 percent of profits. It set up an external board, made up of Ben & Jerry's loyalists, which was charged with protecting its culture. The board could sue Unilever and did not answer directly to its parent company.

After a rocky transition period, in the years since the acquisition Ben & Jerry's has grown more significant as a business and as an agent of social change. It continues to sell literally tons of ice cream in a growing assortment of flavors and markets around the world. More significantly, it continues to be publicly very active and supportive about various social causes like gun violence prevention, environmental protection, LGBTQ rights, sustainable farming, and campaign finance reform. The company has not been shy about wading deeply into divisive and controversial issues, such as racial injustice after the horrific killing of George Floyd, and various policies of the Trump administration. And it has also openly tied its products to its social causes. For example, its Rainforest Crunch ice cream uses responsibly sourced ingredients from the Amazon and has raised awareness about deforestation through its packaging and marketing, and it changed its New York Super Fudge Chunk to Pecan Resist in protest against the Trump administration's policies that harmed women, minorities, and immigrants.

More significantly, Ben & Jerry's may have played a role in motivating its giant parent company, Unilever, to become more socially active and socially conscious in the way it operates its business.[3] In 2010, ten years after its acquisition of Ben & Jerry's, Unilever established the Unilever Sustainable Living Plan (USLP)—according to its website, "to become the world's most sustainable business. To prove that growth doesn't have to come at the expense of people and planet. To show that business can be a force for good—through actions, not just words."[4] In the first decade under the USLP, Unilever "achieved gender balance in management globally, with 51 percent women in managerial roles, up from 38 percent in 2010," uses 100 percent renewable grid electricity in all of its manufacturing, and continues to make progress on issues like water conservation, sustainable sourcing, workplace inclusion, and greenhouse emissions.[5]

In 2019, Unilever CEO Alan Jope initiated plans to align each of the company's brands with a purpose beyond profit, stating, "We are committed to all our brands having a purpose—we will give them time to identify what this is and how they can take meaningful action. . . . If a brand can't find its purpose, we may sell it."[6] For example, Unilever's Dove soap products focused on female empowerment with its prominent global "Real Beauty" advertisement campaign, which highlights the company's products but also partners with organizations like World Association of Girl Guides and Girl Scouts to help girls develop self-confidence.[7]

Unilever's bold, comprehensive approach has attracted attention, both positive and negative. Every social engagement effort that worked led to praise and a halo effect for the affiliated product. Conversely, every engagement that seemed disingenuous received a swift backlash and hurt the product's brand reputation. More significantly, every quarter of lackluster earnings brought more criticism about its corporate social efforts and also brought talk of management change and possible takeovers.

Not every business is a Ben & Jerry's or a Unilever, nor should they be. Part of the beauty and genius of business is that it can manifest in forms and functions that are limited only by the imaginations and dreams of entrepreneurs and executives. Nevertheless, the experiences of Ben & Jerry's and Unilever can shed light on the future of corporate social activism. Their story highlights the local and global growth of this new business of change, as well as the new attention and scrutiny it would attract to companies and causes.

MORE LOCAL AND MORE GLOBAL

There will be more corporate social activism, locally and globally, because of the larger trends of growing business power and rising activism against longstanding wrongs by a new generation of consumers, stakeholders, shareholders, and citizens.

Businesses, large and small, will engage more in their local communities on issues of national and local importance. While large national businesses attract most of the attention on issues of corporate social activism, small businesses and individual outlets of larger companies make up the social fabric of the everyday lives of people and their neighborhoods. Starbucks is a giant corporation based in Seattle, with over thirty thousand outlets around the world, but your Starbucks café with your friendly barista is part of your community. As such, the issues that affect you, your barista, and your café are going to be the issues that you would want to see that café and its parent company engage in as a cause. And thus, in response to the desires and expectations of their customers, employees, and communities, businesses are likely to engage more in social issues of local relevance and significance.

In 2017, when hundreds of thousands of people were protesting then president Trump's executive orders on immigration, a small group of Yemeni Americans who operated delis and bodegas in New York City decided to close their stores in solidarity as an act of protest, since their ancestral country was among those whose citizens were now barred from immigrating into the United States.[8] This was a remarkable act of local corporate social activism, because New Yorkers will tell you that their local bodega or neighborhood deli simply does not close. These small local businesses do not close for blizzards, power outages, mass protests, transit strikes, or pandemics. They simply do not close; they are the lifeblood and hub of many neighborhoods. They are the place one goes to for the daily newspaper, a cup of coffee, a bagel, or a screwdriver to fix a broken door. Yet hundreds of them closed as an act of protest, costing themselves much-needed sales, but also raising awareness for an issue important to their local community.

With the rise of corporate social activism, global and local businesses will be compelled to care more about those populations and issues closest to them.

At the same time, while its efforts will be more localized, corporate social activism will also grow more global as it touches local communities around the world. Many of the social issues that animate activism do not stop at the borders of countries, any more than the businesses of many large companies stop at the borders of countries. Global supply chains and marketplaces will be implicated in a wide range of social issues and social activism. Issues like climate change, environmental protection, racial injustice, gender equality, income inequality, and LGBTQ rights are not just American issues; they are global issues. They are human issues. They are issues that affect consumers, stakeholders, shareholders, and citizens across the globe. They are also issues where businesses, particularly those with a global footprint, can have a positive impact across countries in many ways that nation-states constrained by principles of sovereignty simply cannot.

Moreover, the global nature of business will necessarily mean that corporate social activism will find itself exported, transplanted, and adopted in other countries in the same way that good business practices in the United States, Japan, Germany, and other countries are becoming commonplace for businesses around the world. While the core ideas and principles of corporate social activism will travel across the globe, they will adapt to local customs and practices, in much the same way that American management or accounting practices influence European standards, or Japanese auto manufacturing methods helped shape American car manufacturers.

MORE ATTENTION AND MORE CONTENTION

The growth of corporate social activism will attract more attention and scrutiny. Positive impact and success stories will be amplified by activists, supporters, and the businesses themselves. False starts and failings will also be amplified by activists, critics, and other businesses. This growing spotlight on businesses will lead them to be more thoughtful and sensitive to social issues in their businesses and communities. The increased attention will also lead businesses to be more accountable to their communities and stakeholders beyond merely financial measures. As businesses increasingly position themselves as good, socially engaged citizens, any failing—real or perceived—will receive wider consumer and public scrutiny.

In 2018, Starbucks—which regularly touts itself as a progressive, socially responsible business—found itself embroiled in controversy when two Black men were arrested at one of its cafés in Philadelphia for simply sitting down after being refused access to the restroom because they had not made a purchase. A Starbucks employee called the police after the men refused to leave, even though they were there to meet someone. The incident was captured on video and went viral on social media a few hours after it happened. Millions of people viewed it. #BoycottStarbucks quickly trended on Twitter.[9] Starbucks CEO Kevin Johnson publicly apologized to the men and affirmed Starbucks' opposition to racial discrimination. Starbuck closed all of its stores for training, initiated a review of its practices, and changed its in-store policies.

Part of the strong criticism that Starbucks elicited from the controversy came because the company has long positioned itself as a caring, compassionate, and socially conscious corporation. Hence many people saw the incident as an act of corporate hypocrisy.

Whether Starbucks and all of its thirty thousand-plus outlets should bear the stain and scrutiny brought by one employee at one café is debatable. What is less debatable is that this is the new normal when it comes to corporate scrutiny and accountability in the age of socially conscious consumers and citizens, with social media platforms that can reach millions instantaneously.

In 2021, the Republican legislature and governor of Georgia passed a new voting law that made it harder for many of its citizens to vote, particularly those in urban and suburban Democratic districts. In response to the law, many businesses and executives, including those at Delta Airlines and Coca-Cola—two of Georgia's most prominent businesses—and leading executives like Kenneth Chenault and Ken Frazier publicly spoke out against the law and rallied opposition support from other prominent businesses. These actions were motivated in large part by hearing loud outcries from employees, customers, and activists. Major League Baseball even moved its All-Star Game from Atlanta to Denver as an act of protest against the new law.

Not surprisingly, these corporate actions drew sharp criticism from local and national political leaders who supported the new Georgia law. But these actions also drew criticism from some activists who opposed the law, because they thought that certain business leaders did not condemn the law strongly or swiftly enough. Beyond criticism, Delta, Coca-Cola, Major League Baseball, and other companies who protested the law all received threats of counter-boycotts and punitive regulations.

As corporate social activism grows more common, so will the attention, scrutiny, and criticism for both capitalists and activists, as well as their businesses and causes. The growing spotlight will raise tough questions about the efficacy and merits of this new business of change. Every false start or failed attempt will be cast by critics as evidence of a fundamental failure or defect of this fusion of capitalism and activism. The growing spotlight and scrutiny can also enhance this new business of change, just as failures in businesses offer valuable lessons and insights for future businesses.

The new business of social change made possible by contemporary corporate social activism will continue to grow, mature, and evolve over time. While there is much about how it will develop and change over time that remains unknown, what is known is that it will continue, it will become both more local and more global, and it will attract more attention and scrutiny. The injection of local considerations with global, cultural issues will make contemporary corporate social activism much more complicated, interesting, and impactful for years to come.

CHAPTER 10

The Journey Forward

S OME OF THE FIRST MAPS IN THE WORLD can be traced to caves in present-day Southwestern France dating back to 14,500 BCE. They were maps of places uncharted and untraveled. They were maps of bright stars in the heavens. They were maps of hope and promise that early humans aspired to progress toward someday.

Similarly, the paths ahead for capitalists and activists engaging in this new business of social change present uncharted and untraveled territory filled with hope and promise. Nevertheless, the journey will not always be swift, smooth, or straight. There will be many mistakes and missteps, false starts and failures, difficulties and discomforts. Just as no meaningful, lasting progress is gained without real struggle, and just as no successful sustainable business is established without stumbles, fusing capitalism and activism together as a force for greater social good will not always be easy. But with effort, persistence, and faith, good intentions and well-placed ambitions can turn into purpose and practice, just as has been the case in the long, distinguished separate histories of activism and capitalism.

TIPS FOR THE JOURNEY FORWARD

There are no good roadmaps for the paths ahead, but the early history of this new business of change offers guideposts and first principles to keep in mind as one endeavors to chart and travel in this new territory at the crossroads of business and activism. The following are ten tips for activists and capitalists as they journey forward.

1. Establish and Publish a Purpose-Driven Mission Statement

Capitalists and activists should each establish and publish a purpose-driven mission statement to focus their intentions and their powers. The mission statement would serve as a grounding, foundational document that centers and gives meaning to their work. Human beings are drawn to and motivated by a purpose larger than themselves, be that a family, a tribe, a community, a company, or a cause. After establishing the mission statement, it should be published. Publishing the mission statement not only shares the group's animating creation story with the world, but it also creates an accountability mechanism that allows internal and external actors to hold the businesses and the activists accountable should they deviate too far from their core mission.

This tip is particularly relevant for business leaders who have long seen the purpose of their business purely and narrowly as profit generation. Executives and entrepreneurs should give serious consideration to establishing and publishing a corporate purpose beyond the amoral pursuit of profit, and one that authentically articulates their core values and missions. For example, in 2018, BlackRock, one of the largest and most influential institutional investors in the world, asked corporations to publicly articulate a long-term corporate purpose that accounts for their social and economic impact beyond profits alone.[1]

Businesses should establish a purpose-driven mission not as a matter of superficial public relations, but as a matter of establishing a core identity. And they should authentically communicate that mission to better connect with the public and key stakeholders of their business. Daniel Pink, in his best-selling book *Drive: The Surprising Truth About What Motivates Us*, observed:

> We're learning that the profit motive, potent though it is, can be an insufficient impetus for both individuals and organizations. An equally powerful source of energy, one we've often neglected or dismissed as unrealistic, is what we might call the "purpose motive." Many entrepreneurs, executives, and investors are realizing that the best performing companies stand for something and contribute to the world.[2]

This purpose-driven mission could be incredibly powerful in motivating employees to be more productive, customers to be more loyal, and investors to be more patient with the company. This does not mean that for-profit businesses should abdicate the pursuit of profits or the metrics of financial success. Rather, this means that businesses should be able to articulate their profit-seeking purposes in a comprehensive, meaningful manner that better accounts for the social interests and norms expected of today's best businesses, which in turn may actually lead to superior financial performance. There is growing evidence that companies that focus on goals beyond narrow financial metrics actually perform better financially.[3] Purpose beyond pure profit turns out to be more profitable in the long run.

2. Focus Internally, Then Locally, Then Beyond

Capitalists and activists should first focus their collective efforts on the communities nearest to them before expanding outward. As such, capitalists and activists should focus their resources and efforts internally, then locally, then beyond.

Capitalists, in particular, should begin their socially enhancing efforts internally within their own businesses. There are activists in every business, animating for change and progress within the firm itself. Businesses should work with these internal activists. To start, businesses should treat their employees and contractors well. Pay them fairly, give them safe working conditions, and provide them with more than adequate benefits so that they can truly share in the gains of the business. It is hard to appear like you genuinely want to be a good corporate citizen if you cannot or will not take care of the very people that make your success as a business possible.

Next, capitalists and activists should focus their resources and efforts locally prior to expanding their energies to a broader geographic scope. The surrounding neighborhoods usually consist of key supporters, customers, and employees, as well as critics. Having a positive impact on these key constituencies that know you best could boost morale and momentum to expand the efforts. For instance, during the COVID-19 pandemic in 2020, Philadelphia-based Comcast, working with local activists and officials, provided free, reliable high-speed Wi-Fi at various hot spots in Philadelphia for local residents and students during their time of need. This effort engendered a great deal of goodwill for a company that has not always left its customers and the public with a great impression.

For capitalists, focusing locally involves not just good deeds in the community; it also involves paying their fair share of taxes and working with government to contain negative externalities from their businesses. It is hard, if not downright hypocritical, to say that you care about your local community in one sense, then turn around and evade fair tax payments and reasonable regulations that would enhance the welfare of that community.

By focusing internally, then locally, then globally, capitalists and activists can position themselves to succeed where they are often most familiar and comfortable, with the communities closest to them. Those communities are usually the ones they know the best, the ones with key stakeholders, and the ones that can generate the biggest, fastest impact. The communities closest to them are also often the ones that make their success possible. This is akin to the home field advantage in sports. Focusing internally and locally first also has the benefit of learning from mistakes in a more forgiving and familiar environment and then using lessons to scale more broadly. As with many things in life, proximity matters.

3. Pair Lofty Goals with Actionable Objectives

Capitalists and activists should translate their noble principles into tangible practices. Justice, equality, fairness, and a greener world are all noble goals worth pursuing, but these ideals in and of themselves are insufficient. They should be coupled with concrete, achievable objectives, so that businesses and activists can see that their efforts and resources are planting seeds that bear fruit. In the absence of clear, actionable objectives, social activism can seem like a Sisyphean task without meaning or possibility of success.

Lofty goals are necessary to keep our aims high, but actionable objectives are like rungs of a ladder. They make progress seem possible and real. They make the effort seem worth it. These incremental steps upward give capitalists and activists reason to continue in their efforts, and they create momentum for progress.

In setting forth actionable objectives, activists and capitalists, in particular, should make sure those objectives are consistent with their other actions, whenever possible. It would be foolhardy and hypocritical for a business to try to promote cleaner water and air to its community, only to also be lobbying against reasonable regulations that could help make that possible in a sensible manner. That said, contradictory activities may be inevitable in some circumstances, given the complex and expansive nature of many large businesses.

There might be no greater advocate for the grand and high goals of justice and equality in the United States than Dr. Martin Luther King. Yet King translated his quest for these goals into a pursuit of tangible practices and policies like voting rights, antidiscrimination laws, higher minimum wages, and universal basic income. And throughout his life and beyond, the civil rights movement he started has worked to achieve these concrete goals as a means of creating a more just and equal society.

4. Be Pragmatic

Capitalists and activists should approach their work by recognizing the world as it *is*, even as they try to make it as it *should* be. Capitalists and activists can embrace more pragmatism in their shared efforts for progress while maintaining fidelity to their core values and high ideals. Being pragmatic means recognizing systemic flaws, shortcomings, and outright wrongs, yet nevertheless trying to make it work better. Being pragmatic means embracing reality in all of its contradictions, complexities, and ambiguities of the present and the past, while keeping your eyes on the prize for the future.

Being pragmatic in corporate social activism means that both capitalists and activists should be open to working with parties that they do not wholeheartedly embrace on every issue in order to make progress on larger goals and objectives. Activists might disagree with the Koch brothers' conservative, libertarian politics but still see them as valuable partners on the issue of criminal justice or immigration reform. A company might not agree with every tactic of Black Lives Matter activists, but nevertheless work earnestly with them on the issue of racial justice, so that progress is made.

Being pragmatic often means being both urgent and patient, and open to accepting compromises and less-than-full measures in order to take forward steps that make larger shifts possible. In the American civil rights movement in the 1960s, activists, capitalists, and policymakers made significant strides over much time and through great struggle by being incredibly pragmatic. Civil rights activists of that era formed alliances with people and parties that they personally found problematic, and they accepted compromise solutions as a means toward the next station for their goals and objectives.

Progress often requires pragmatism, not purity or perfection. We cannot work only with individuals and institutions that we agree with on every single position on every issue across every single point on a long timeline. While purity and perfection might be satisfying in fleeting moments in the echo chambers of social media or academia, the world is too complicated and its challenges are too great for us to needlessly dismiss or righteously cancel potentially credible partners and solutions that can help effectuate social progress.

Being pragmatic is not surrender. Being pragmatic is not cynicism. Being pragmatic is not selling out. In truth, being pragmatic is often the only real path to progress in an uncertain, complicated world.

5. Go Beyond Corporate Social Responsibility

Capitalists and activists should think beyond traditional conceptions of corporate social responsibility. Traditional corporate social responsibility programs and efforts may be too company-focused and insular. While many of these programs—which exist at all major corporations—are commendable, they may be insufficient to meet the needs and expectations of a changing society with awakened shareholders, stakeholders, consumers, and citizens. A 2020 Axios Harris poll indicated that people today strongly want and expect their businesses and business leaders to engage with important social issues: "72% say they invest in companies whose values they admire, 83% would work for or recommend a family member to work for a company whose values they share and 58% will boycott brands that don't stand for racial equality."[4]

The traditional, self-facing corporate social responsibility program concentrates its efforts largely on creating firm cultures and practices that reflect a caring, compassionate business. This is important and good, but it may also be too passive and self-centered. It is akin to having the best fire protection for your house while the rest of the neighborhood is on fire.

Rather than working within the confines of only improving the firms themselves, capitalists and activists should work to update old programs so that they become more proactive, more outward-facing, more inclusive, and more engaged with local communities and the world at large. They should do so not only because their stakeholders demand it, but also because ultimately it is how they can have the biggest impact on their businesses and the world.

6. Engage in Public Policy and Politics

Capitalists and activists should work smartly to engage with public policymakers and government institutions in their efforts. This engagement should happen at the national, regional, and local levels. While national politics and public policy debates too often capture most of our media attention, the politics that affect people's daily lives the most often happen at the local and regional levels. Local and regional politics and policymaking do not receive wide media coverage, but these actually can have the deepest impact on people's lives. While contemporary corporate social activism arose in part because of dissatisfaction with dysfunctional government, it is no substitute for good, effective government and public policy in a democratic society. The new business of change can fill gaps between callous private markets and unresponsive government institutions, but it cannot replace government.

Many of the most persistent social problems are too big, too complicated, and too costly for corporate social activism to solve on its own. Climate change, racial injustice, income inequality, and a whole host of social challenges all require government resources and action. Support from public policy and government institutions is not just desirable, but essential.

The Gates Foundation, one of the wealthiest philanthropic organizations in the world, had an endowment of around $50 billion in 2021.[5] That figure pales in comparison to the annual budgets of government entities. New York City has an annual budget of about $88 billion. Cities like Philadelphia and Los Angeles spend about $10 billion a year on city operations. The U.S. federal government spends about $5.8 trillion annually. The U.S. Department of Health and Human Services (HHS) alone has an annual budget of over \$1.2 trillion. All the money in the Gates Foundation could barely pay for 4 percent of all the funds that are spent by HHS each year.

Government support is necessary for social change, if for no other reason than its unmatched financial resources. Beyond funding, government support is necessary because only government can give the official state imprimatur of law and official recognition, especially when issues implicate foreign policy or the jurisdictions of another sovereign.

At best, corporate social activism can fill in near-term gaps exposed by the failings of private markets and dysfunctional government, and can serve as a catalyst for meaningful government action. Regardless of the effectiveness of capitalists and activists, for social change to be truly impactful and lasting, public policy and political institutions must be engaged. And they must be engaged in a manner consistent with the lofty goals and values of the organization or movement.

While politicians like to say that some issues are "more than politics" or "beyond politics," if they were being honest with us and themselves, they would confess that the truly important and consequential issues of our time need politics and the political process. Racial justice, voting rights, climate change, income inequality, and affordable health care are simply not issues that capitalists and activists can solve on their own. If those involved in the new business of change want to have broad and deep impact, they should thoughtfully and compassionately engage with public institutions of government, be it through legislation, regulation, litigation, elections, or some combination of all of the above.

7. Leverage Comparative Advantages

Capitalists and activists need to better wield their comparative advantages and core competencies to advance their causes. Rather than trying to work on a host of issues in a variety of disconnected ways, they should concentrate their efforts. This is particularly true for businesses that feel compelled to work on a wide range of social issues from various constituencies. While they should contribute to as many causes as they deem worthy, they should try to concentrate their social activism on a few key issues.

Rather than simply writing checks and outsourcing social activism efforts on a wide range of issues, corporations should thoughtfully focus and prioritize their capital and expertise on efforts where they can offer a comparative advantage. For instance, UPS's social activism efforts should leverage its expertise in delivery and logistics; Airbnb's efforts should focus on housing; and Bank of America's efforts should focus on finance.

By focusing and prioritizing on areas of comparative advantage and core competencies, businesses can also better align their social activism with their business interests where there exists a clear mutually beneficial nexus between the two. For example, in 2021, Uber and Lyft partnered with the federal government to provide free rides to and from COVID vaccine sites to encourage vaccinations, to everyone's benefit. These efforts also benefited Lyft and Uber by creating safer markets for their drivers and attracting new customers for their services.

8. Create Partnerships, Not Sponsorships

Capitalists and activists should view one another not as sponsors, benefactors, or contractors but as partners. Working together as partners will likely create mutual benefits, cross-learning opportunities, and greater impact for their shared cause.

For activists, collaborating with capitalists as partners will give them access to significant expertise, connections, and resources that may turn out to be much more valuable than merely receiving a donation. Seeing capitalists and their companies as partners and treating them as such will also allow activists to help inform, shape, and influence private institutions in ways that they otherwise could not with a mere sponsorship or endorsement.

For capitalists, working with activists as partners, not as contractors or beneficiaries, will allow them to unlock key insights about a social issue and create a deeper impact than they might otherwise gain. Seeing and treating activists as partners will also give capitalists more influence over the particular strategies and tactics of the activism. This may be especially important to businesses; since they are sensitive to the reputational effects of social activism, they would want to make certain that the tactics and strategies of the activism on one issue or another aligns with their institutional values.

9. Measure and Disclose

Capitalists and activists should collect data on their efforts and disclose them to the public, not just as a function of accountability, transparency, and legal compliance, but also as a function of good management. They should set clear benchmarks for their efforts and see how effective (or ineffective) they are at meeting their goals. They should publicly disclose their data and benchmarks so that the public can serve as a check of accountability.

Data-driven management will help inform activists and capitalists as to how best to deploy their limited resources and efforts, so they are not unduly swayed by heart-wrenching anecdotes, justified passions, or the strategies and tactics of the past for an issue or cause. *How effective is a boycott or march? When is the best time to stage a march? How much reach does a hashtag campaign have on an issue? What is the most impactful way to spend a dollar on this issue or that cause? How much impact did our last efforts have on the targeted communities? How many lives were saved?* These are the types of questions that data can help answer for capitalists and activists.

There is some truth in the business mantra that what is measured gets managed. While this data-driven management approach has grown quite prevalent and useful in the business world, it has not taken the same hold in activism, but it could prove to be similarly useful. Having said that, it is also important to note that data gathering and benchmarking can be incredibly difficult on some social issues and challenges. Moreover, data, with their inevitable underlying biases and defects, should inform corporate social activism, but not necessarily dictate it. The sociologist William Bruce Cameron famously remarked, "Not everything that can be counted counts. Not everything that counts can be counted."[6]

10. Review, Reform, Renew, or Relinquish

Capitalists and activists should establish a predetermined mechanism of review in their social activism protocols for their efforts and activities, be it annually, quarterly, or some other time interval. A predetermined review mechanism will enable them to assess whether their corporate social activism efforts are effective and impactful, and how better to improve their processes and methods. These mechanisms could take the form of sunset provisions in funding agreements or quarterly financial and efficacy audits. Effective and successful efforts should be renewed and scaled up, where appropriate. Conversely, ineffective programs should be reformed or relinquished, so that resources can be redirected to efforts that work.

In the absence of a predetermined review mechanism, status quo bias and other human factors can make it incredibly difficult for capitalists and activists to deviate from a less optimal path toward a better one. The importance of some of the social issues that animate corporate social activism could also make it particularly difficult for passionate individuals to relinquish means that turn out to be unworkable or ineffective, despite wonderful intentions. As such, predetermined review mechanisms will make some of these difficult transitions easier.

Ultimately, predetermined mechanisms for review and reform will allow capitalists and activists to better adapt and adjust to a dynamic, rapidly changing society to maximize their impact.

KEY GUIDEPOSTS

The journey ahead for corporate social activism will be an exciting, interesting, yet challenging one, as much of the terrain remains unexplored and uncharted. While there are no roadmaps or guidebooks, capitalists and activists engaging in contemporary corporate social activism would do well to follow the preceding ten tips for how best to navigate this new territory. They are assembled here in a list for convenient reference:

1. **Establish and publish a purpose-driven mission statement.**

2. **Focus internally, then locally, then beyond.**

3. **Pair lofty goals with actionable objectives.**

4. **Be pragmatic.**

5. **Go beyond corporate social responsibility.**

6. **Engage in public policy and politics.**

7. **Leverage comparative advantages.**

8. **Create partnerships, not sponsorships.**

9. **Measure and disclose.**

10. **Review, reform, renew, or relinquish.**

Admittedly, some of the tips can be perceived as competing, complementary, and crosscutting. They should be adapted and customized to suit the particular needs and circumstance of an organization, issue, or cause. Further, these are *tips*—not rules— for the road ahead. They are intended to serve as guideposts— not roadblocks—for capitalists and activists working in the new business of social change. They are intended to help activists and capitalists move forward toward achieving their goals and objectives, toward meaningful progress.

We Are More Than

WHO IS THE GREATEST BASKETBALL PLAYER of all time? Among basketball fans, this question generates a ton of debate. More often than not, the debate has converged on two names: Michael Jordan and LeBron James.

The case for Jordan is straightforward and strong. Six-time NBA champion. Six NBA Finals MVP awards. Five league-wide MVP awards. Ten-time scoring champion. One Defensive Player of the Year Award. Countless gravity-defying moves and clutch baskets. To say nothing of the iconic sneakers and how he fundamentally revolutionized the game from one about big men to one about small guards who could fly.

The case for LeBron James is just as straightforward and strong. Four NBA championships with three different teams. Four-time NBA Finals MVP. Four league-wide MVP awards.

One-time scoring champion. One-time assist leader. To say nothing of how he built on Jordan's legacy and revolutionized the definition of a basketball superstar during an era when the game and its players became faster and more skilled than ever. At the time of this writing and the end of the 2020–2021 NBA season, James continued to play basketball at the highest level at the age of thirty-six, an age where most players have retired or been relegated to a supporting role.

In terms of business, Jordan and James are both incredibly successful capitalists. Jordan is a billionaire and the principal owner of the NBA Charlotte Hornets. His Jordan Brand under Nike is worth an estimated $10 billion.[1] He also has a variety of business interests and endorsements worth millions of dollars. Jordan during his playing days was arguably the most famous person in the world, and a favorite brand ambassador of corporate America.

James has an estimated net worth of $275 million and growing.[2] In addition to being one of the highest-paid athletes in the world, James is an astute investor and entrepreneur. James and his partners own LRMR, a sports-marketing company, as well as SpringHill Entertainment, which produces movies and television shows.

Where these two basketball icons diverge is in their approaches to activism, especially during their playing days. Jordan largely avoided commenting on controversial, social issues during his career. James, in contrast, has used his platform to be an outspoken agent of social change. To lift up young children in his hometown of Akron, Ohio, James and his family foundation started the I Promise School. Using his business prowess, James also partnered with the University of Akron and JPMorgan Chase to provide free tuition to the university for every qualified graduate of an Akron public high school. During the unrest and protests that followed the killings of unarmed Black men and women like Trayvon Martin, Eric Garner, Michael Brown, George Floyd, and Breonna Taylor, James spoke out and demonstrated with his teammates. During the Trump presidency, James often spoke out against the president's actions and policies.

In 2020, after the police shooting of Jacob Blake in Milwaukee, James led NBA players in discussions with the league and owners to act on racial justice. The discussions resulted in immediate donations to numerous civil rights organizations, a public campaign to raise racial justice awareness, and the formation of foundations and task forces to address the issue within the league and beyond. Most significantly, James and his peers convinced team owners to convert their arenas to be used as polling sites for the 2020 election. James also formed the More Than a Vote initiative to register and get millions of people to the polls for the 2020 election. This made it much easier for millions of Americans to vote and turn out in numbers unseen in decades, and in the middle of a pandemic.

While James's efforts brought him much acclaim, they also brought him scorn and criticism. At one point, then president Trump even publicly admonished James in a tweet, and conservative television host Laura Ingraham told him to "shut up and dribble." His retort to his critics was a post to his over ninety-five million Instagram followers of an image with the words "I AM MORE THAN AN ATHLETE."

When *Time* magazine named James its 2020 Athlete of the Year, it wrote:

> It was James, heir to Jordan on the court and in the boardroom, who established a new paradigm, in which commercial clout exists alongside political principle. He remains one of the world's top pitchmen. . . . And he has laid waste to the dated notion

that political and social engagement is some sort
of distraction for athletes. In 2020, James led the
NBA in assists, for the first time in his career, before
winning the NBA championship and his fourth
Finals MVP award, at age 35. Athletes can now
bring their full humanity to their games, insisting
that their identities be recognized and rejecting the
notion that their athleticism is all that matters.[3]

Much of the world wanted to cast LeBron James narrowly
into one role, into one tribe, and he refused to let them do so. He
embraced his entire humanity and all of his multitudes to impact
the world.

A BROADER, RICHER VIEW OF US

While none of us can be LeBron James, we all can learn from his
refusal to be pigeonholed into one role or tribe. Just as James is
more than an athlete, we all are more than. We are more than a
child, a parent, a student, a job, an ethnicity, an age, or any narrowly constructed box that we or others may want to cage ourselves in. We are more than capable of just being one role, of
doing one thing. We are more than capable of being good capitalists and good activists. We are more than capable of making
a meaningful difference in our communities through capitalism
and activism.

For too long, activism and capitalism have been viewed as
distinct ideas manifesting in different activities between two
different groups of people. They are often viewed irreconcil-
ably, in black and white, as either the selfless crusade of a larger
social cause or the selfish pursuit of a narrow individual profit.
In reality, these demarcations and divisions are often arbitrarily

self-imposed, and thus they can be self-removed. We all can do better to embrace our multiplicity of roles and capacities to effectuate progress in society using tools of activism, capitalism, and our whole humanity during a new era of change.

Contemporary corporate social activism offers not only a new path to social progress, but also a new perspective for our roles in making this progress real. It offers us a way to see ourselves in a broader, more diverse, and more complete fashion—beyond narrow definitions of activist and capitalist—as a complete person.

BEYOND EITHER/OR

Society often perpetuates a dichotomy between working for the public interest or working for private gain. This notion presupposes that either one can choose to work for the public interest by entering into government service or the nonprofit world *or* one can choose to work for private gain by going to work for a corporation. Furthermore, the public interest path is seen by many as more noble and socially positive. Year after year, hundreds of thousands of students exit high schools, colleges, law schools, medical schools, business schools, and graduate schools making life and work decisions based on this dichotomy. While this dichotomy may contain a kernel of truth, it is largely false in light of many changing expectations, policies, and practices in the worlds of business and activism. This falsehood is more obvious now than ever, given the rise of contemporary corporate social activism.

People can choose to do good for society and the public's interests regardless of where they work. With the rise of corporate social activism, working with and for corporations can improve the public's interests like never before. Businesses are among the most innovative and powerful engines of economic progress, and they are increasingly becoming vehicles for social progress as well. Although not without their many serious flaws and failings, businesses operating in free markets, through the hard work and ingenuity of the people working with them, have fostered unparalleled wealth creation, economic growth, and technological innovation. Through jobs, goods, and services, corporations have directly created many economic benefits for society. And using their tools, expertise, and resources, they can engage in activism to make a better, more just society as well.

With the rise of corporate social activism, public interest work should mean more than working for the government or a non-profit organization. The new language and rules of social change are becoming more synonymous with the language and rules of business. The young and the young at heart interested in working for the public's interests should consider working at businesses, because corporations are at the forefront of many of the leading social challenges of our time, to say nothing of the direct economic benefits that they create for society through better business practices. For instance, if you care about climate change and environmental protection, you should consider working at the Sierra Club or the Environmental Protection Agency, but you should also consider working on the sustainability efforts at Apple or Walmart, two large global corporations that are making huge consequential commitments to sustainable energy and efforts to expand its use.

THE CAPITALIST AND THE ACTIVIST WITHIN

Old perceptions and divisions of public or private, profit or non-profit, must be stripped away in light of emerging new realities so that the public's interests can be served from every vantage point. The corporate manager who regularly marches for racial justice or organizes for changes within their company is also an activist, just as the community leader who creates and sells merchandise for her cause online is also a capitalist. Working apart or working together, they are both trying to make their communities better. Neither of their pursuits should be discounted, discouraged, or diminished. The old walls dividing outdated notions of public and private, profit and nonprofit must be torn down, if for no other reason than to ensure that society is not deprived of some of the most promising people year after year because they are forced to choose between doing only this or that in the face of tough, persistent societal challenges that require their attention.

Overcoming these persistent yet pressing challenges—for justice, equality, freedom, liberty, dignity, and a sustainable planet—will not be easy. Even when working well, corporate social activism may fall short and disappoint. Its critics and skeptics are understandably hesitant and rightfully mistrusting of its intentions and ends, as history offers many reasons for that cynical worldview. Persuading the doubtful and the pessimistic will be difficult, as it takes a lot to change a person's worldview. And it may take a lot more to even try. Nevertheless, however difficult, the failings of the past and the promise of progress in the future demand that we try anyway.

The timely and timeless challenges that confront us as a society are simply too important, too large, and too complex to be left only to the good, hardworking activists and people in government and the nonprofit sector. These challenges require the creativity, ingenuity, resources, and efforts of the private sector as well as the public sector, those working for nonprofit causes as well as those working for very profitable causes. These challenges require the best of us, of all of us.

In the end, the emergence and evolution of contemporary corporate social activism is in one sense a story of how we can meet and master these old yet urgent challenges in new ways, with new perspectives. It is one of the most consequential stories of business and society in recent history and will remain so for the foreseeable future. The conflicts, collaborations, and complexities between and among capitalists and activists will present some of the most fruitful opportunities and dangerous obstacles for meaningful social progress in our time. All of us will be impacted by this unfolding story. It is an incomplete story. Much of it remains to be written. But it is a hopeful one. It is a story that we all share, and can all help shape together by finding the activist and the capitalist within.

The Capitalist and the Activist

T HANK YOU FOR READING THE BOOK. I hope *The Capitalist and the Activist* has provided you with new insights and changed your perspective on issues relating to business, activism, and social progress.

The following questions and prompts are designed to help you think more and to facilitate discussions with others about issues covered in the book. The questions and prompts are written broadly to engender a wide range of conversations and exchanges.

1. What was your reaction to reading *The Capitalist and the Activist*? Did any chapter or story surprise or move you?

2. How do you define capitalism? What do you see as some of the chief characteristics of capitalism? Do you see yourself as a capitalist?

3. How do you define activism? What do you see as some of the chief characteristics of activism? Do you see yourself as an activist?

4. When was your last act of activism? When was your last act of capitalism?

5. How would you explain corporate social activism to someone who is unfamiliar with the idea?

6. Are your consumption choices significantly influenced by the social positions of the businesses that create the products and services you seek? Are price and convenience greater factors than social activism when you shop?

7. Can activism and capitalism be completely reconciled? What do you see as potential areas of tension?

8. How has technology like social media and online fundraising platforms changed activism and capitalism? How have these developments impacted social change?

9. What should be the primary goal(s) of corporations?

10. How should the various stakeholders of a business be prioritized? What are the values that drive your ranking of stakeholders?

11. What do you believe is motivating business leaders to speak out and move so publicly on social issues not directly related to their business? Customers? Employees? Shareholders? Media? Morals? Civic duty? Profits?

12. How can we understand corporations' lobbying for lower taxes and less regulation vis-à-vis their words and deeds on other social issues like racial justice, LGBTQ rights, climate change, and gun violence?

13. If U.S. politics were not so partisan and dysfunctional, would you expect the same level of corporate social activism?

14. Do you see corporate campaign contributions and lobbying as critical factors contributing to a broken system of government? Should business work to reduce their own influence in government?

15. Should corporations prioritize fixing our broken democratic institutions in addition to or in lieu of working on discrete social causes and issues?

16. What do you think are the toughest social issues for businesses to engage in as part of corporate social activism? Why?

17. What do you see as some of the chief drawbacks of corporate social activism? Do the costs outweigh the benefits?

18. Should government regulate the social activism efforts of businesses? If so, how? Prohibitions? Limitations? Disclosures?

19. Can the principles and practices of corporate social activism that originate in the United States be exported to other countries that have different business practices and governmental systems? How can corporate social activism work in autocratic or socialist regimes where state-owned enterprises are more prevalent?

20. How do you see corporate social activism evolving over time? Do you expect to see its influence growing or waning over time?

NOTES

Preface

1. Dennis O'Driscoll, *Stepping Stones: Interviews with Seamus Heaney* (London: Faber & Faber, 2008), 72.

Introduction

1. Tiffany Hsu, "Where Others Fear to Tread, Bank Imposes Gun Measures," *New York Times* (Mar. 23, 2018), B1.

2. Tiffany Hsu, "Gunmakers Facing Limits from Another Major Lender," *New York Times* (Apr. 11, 2018), B3.

3. *See* Laura M. Holson, "Dick's Will Destroy Unsold Military-Style Weapons," *New York Times* (Apr. 19, 2018), B3; Tiffany Hsu, "Protests Are Common. The Boycott of the N.R.A. Is Different," *New York Times* (Feb. 28, 2018), A12; Avi Selk, "NRA Lashes Out at Boycott Movement as United, Delta and Other Corporations Cut Ties," *Washington Post* (Feb. 25, 2018, 10:41 AM), https://www.washingtonpost.com/news/morning-mix/wp/2018/02/24/united-and-delta-cut-ties-to-nra-as-boycott-movement-spreads-to-global-corporations/?noredirect=on&utm_term=.4dce737972a7.

Chapter 1

1. Zoe Thomas and Tim Swift, "Who Is Martin Shkreli—'The Most Hated Man in America'?," *BBC* (Aug. 4, 2017), https://www.bbc.com/news/world-us-canada-34331761; Eric Owles, "The Making of Martin Shkreli as 'Pharma Bro,'" *New York Times*: DealBook (June 22, 2017), https://www.nytimes.com/2017/06/22/business/dealbook/martin-shkreli-pharma-bro-drug-prices.html.

2. Dan Diamond, "Martin Shkreli Admits He Messed Up: He Should've Raised Prices Even Higher," *Forbes* (Dec. 3, 2015, 12:55 PM), https://www.forbes.com/sites/dandiamond/2015/12/03/what-martin-shkreli-says-now-i-shouldve-raised-prices-higher/#7ff4b0e31362; Bethany McLean, "Everything You Know About Martin Shkreli is Wrong—or Is It?," *Vanity Fair* (Dec. 18, 2015), https://www.vanityfair.com/news/2015/12/martin-shkreli-pharmaceuticals-ceo-interview.

3. Diamond, "Martin Shkreli Admits He Messed Up."

4. Jane S. Smith, *Patenting the Sun: Polio and the Salk Vaccine*, (New York: William Morrow, 1990), 13.

5. "How Much Money Did Jonas Salk Potentially Forfeit By Not Patenting the Polio Vaccine?," *Forbes* (Aug. 9, 2012, 12:40 PM), https://www.forbes.com/sites/quora/2012/08/09/how-much-money-did-jonas-salk-potentially-forfeit-by-not-patenting-the-polio-vaccine/#7494af2269b8.

6. World Health Organization (WHO), *Cost-effectiveness Evidence—A Case Study*, 2, https://www.euro.who.int/__data/assets/pdf_file/0005/345686/Case-study-US-polio.pdf.

7. *Dodge v. Ford Motor Company*, 204 Mich. 459, 507, 170 N.W. 668, 684 (Mich. 1919).

8. Lynn A. Stout, *The Shareholder Value Myth: How Putting Shareholders First Harms Investors, Corporations, and the Public* (San Francisco: Berrett-Koehler, 2012), 8.

9. *See* E. Merrick Dodd, Jr., "For Whom Are Corporate Managers Trustees?," *Harvard Law Review* 45 (1932), 1145, 1148.

10. Herman E. Krooss, *Executive Opinion: What Business Leaders Said and Thought on Economic Issues, 1920s-1960s* (New York: Doubleday, 1970), 52.

11. Milton Friedman, "A Friedman Doctrine—The Social Responsibility of Business Is to Increase Its Profits," *New York Times* (Sept. 13, 1970), https://www.nytimes.com/1970/09/13/archives/a-friedman-doctrine-the-social-responsibility-of-business-is-to.html.

12. Ibid.

13. *See*, e.g., Bayless Manning, "Corporate Power and Individual Freedom: Some General Analysis and Particular Reservations," 55 *Northwestern University Law Review* 38 (1960), 38–39 (noting growth of corporate power, against which "individual is powerless; his freedom stands in jeopardy").

14. Ibid.

15. Friedman, "A Friedman Doctrine."

16. Lewis F. Powell, Jr., *Powell Memorandum: Attack on American Free Enterprise System* (Lexington City, VA: Washington and Lee University School of Law, 1971), 1, https://www.reuters.com/investigates/special-report/assets/usa -courts-secrecy-lobbyist/powell-memo.pdf.

17. Ronald Reagan, Farewell Address (Jan. 11, 1989), in "Transcript of Reagan's Farewell Address to American People," *New York Times* (Jan. 12, 1989), https://www.nytimes.com/1989/01/12/news/transcript-of-reagan-s-farewell -address-to-american-people.html.

18. Lawrence H. Summers, Opinion, "The Great Liberator," *New York Times* (Nov. 19, 2006), https://www.nytimes.com/2006/11/19/opinion/19summers .html.

19. Andrew Ross Sorkin and Jason Karaian, "Greed Is Good. Except When It's Bad," *New York Times*: DealBook (Sept. 13, 2020), https://www.nytimes.com/ 2020/09/13/business/dealbook/milton-friedman-essay-anniversary.html.

20. Eric W. Orts, "Beyond Shareholders: Interpreting Corporate Constituency Statutes," 61 *George Washington Law Review* 14, 16–28 (1992).

21. Alison Smith, "Fortune 500 Companies Spend More Than $15bn On Corporate Responsibility," *Financial Times* (Oct. 12, 2014), https://www.ft .com/content/95239a6e-4fe0-11e4-a0a4-00144feab7de.

22. *See* William H. Chafe, *Civilities and Civil Rights: Greensboro, North Carolina, and the Black Struggle for Freedom* (Oxford: Oxford University Press, 1980), 71–79. See generally Miles Wolff, *Lunch at the Five and Ten* (Chicago: Ivan R. Dee, 1970).

23. *See* Taylor Branch, *Parting the Waters: America in the King Years 1954–63* (New York: Simon & Schuster, 1989), 32–33, 395; Clay Risen, *The Bill of the Century: The Epic Battle for the Civil Rights Act* (London: Bloomsbury Press, 2014), 63–73, 247.

24. *See* Herbert H. Haines, "Black Radicalization and the Funding of Civil Rights: 1957–1970," *Social Problems* 32, no. 1 (1984): 31–43.

25. Jim Burress, "The Time Coca-Cola Got White Elites in Atlanta to Honor Martin Luther King, Jr.," NPR (Apr. 4, 2015, 9:12 AM), http://www.npr.org/ sections/codeswitch/2015/04/04/397391510/when-corporations-take-the -lead-on-social-change.

26. Lindsey Feitz, "Creating a Multicultural Soul: Avon, Corporate Social Responsibility, and Race in the 1970s," in *The Business of Black Power: Community Development, Capitalism, and Corporate Responsibility in Postwar America*, eds. Laura Warren Hill and Julia Rabig (Rochester: University of Rochester Press, 2012), 116–17.

27. *Heart of Atlanta Motel, Inc. v. United States*, 379 U.S. 241, 261 (1964).

28. Richard Rothstein, *The Color of Law: A Forgotten History of How Our Government Segregated America* (New York: Liveright, 2017), 116–30 (discussing discriminatory practices in housing during the 1960s).

29. "Statement on the Purpose of a Corporation," Business Roundtable (Aug. 19, 2019), https://system.businessroundtable.org/app/uploads/sites/5/2021/02/BRT -Statement-on-the-Purpose-of-a-Corporation-Feburary-2021-compressed.pdf.

Chapter 2

1. *See* David Rothkopf, *Power, Inc.: The Epic Rivalry Between Big Business and Government—And the Reckoning That Lies Ahead* (New York: Farrar, Straus and Giroux, 2013), 195.

2. Allison Stanger, *One Nation Under Contract: The Outsourcing of American Power and the Future of Foreign Policy* (New Haven, CT: Yale University Press, 2011), 1–11.

3. Allison Stanger, "Addicted to Contractors," *Foreign Policy* (Dec. 1, 2009, 6:58 PM), https://foreignpolicy.com/2009/12/01/addicted-to -contractors/.

4. *See*, e.g., Steve Coll, *Private Empire: ExxonMobil and American Power* (London: Penguin, 2013), 19–20.

5. Rothkopf, *Power, Inc.*, 314.

6. *See* "About Us," BlackRock, https://www.blackrock.com/sg/en/about-us (last visited Dec. 27, 2020).

7. *See* Rothkopf, *Power, Inc.*, 310; *Company Facts*, Walmart, http:// corporate.walmart.com/newsroom/company-facts (last visited Dec. 27, 2020).

8. Casey Leins, "These Are the Largest Employers in Every State," *U.S. News & World Report* (Dec. 21, 2018), https://www.usnews.com/news/best -states/articles/2018-12-21/walmart-health-companies-and-universities -are-top-state-employers-study-finds#:~:text=Walmart%20is%20the% 20nation's%20leading,24%2F7%20Wall%20Street%20study.

9. "Number of Monthly Active Facebook Users Worldwide as of 3rd Quarter 2020," Statista, https://www.statista.com/statistics/264810/number-of -monthly-active-facebook-users-worldwide/#:~:text=With%20over%20 2.7%20billion%20monthly,network%20ever%20to%20do%20so (last visited Dec. 27, 2020).

10. Id.

11. "GDP by Country," Worldometer, https://www.worldometers.info/gdp/ gdp-by-country/ (last visited Dec. 27, 2020).

12. *See* "Bailout Recipients," *Pro Publica*, http://projects.propublica.org/bailout/ list (last visited Sept. 21, 2018).

13. Nomi Prins, "The Real Size of the Bailout," *Mother Jones*, https://www .motherjones.com/politics/2009/12/real-size-bailout-treasury-fed/ (last updated Oct. 31, 2009).

14. Sheryl Gay Stolberg and Bill Vlasic, "President Gives a Short Lifeline to Carmakers," *New York Times* (Mar. 30, 2009), A1.

15. Andrew Jacobs, "Despite Claims, Trump Rarely Uses Wartime Law in Battle Against Covid," *New York Times* (Sept. 23, 2020), https://www.nytimes .com/2020/09/22/health/Covid-Trump-Defense-Production-Act.html.

16. Peter Whoriskey et al., "'Doomed to Fail': Why a $4 Trillion Bailout Couldn't Revive the American Economy," *Washington Post* (Oct. 5, 2020), https://www. washingtonpost.com/graphics/2020/business/coronavirus -bailout-spending/.

17. Abraham Lincoln, Fragment On Government, *in Abraham Lincoln: Complete Works, Comprising His Speeches, Letters, State Papers, and Miscellaneous Writings*, eds. John G. Nicolay and John Hay (New York: Century, 1902), 180.

18. *See* Martha Minow, *Partners Not Rivals: Privatization and the Public Good* (Boston: Beacon Press, 2003), 6.

Chapter 3

1. These initial paragraphs drew on the remarkable autobiography of Ann Nixon Cooper. *See* Ann Nixon Cooper with Karen Grigsby Bates, *A Century and Some Change: My Life Before the President Called My Name* (New York: Atria, 2014).

2. "Ann Nixon Cooper, 107; Named in Obama's Victory Speech," *New York Times* (Dec. 23, 2009), A29.

3. Matt Turck, "Can the Bloomberg Terminal Be Toppled?," *Fortune* (Mar. 20, 2014, 4:52 PM), https://fortune.com/2014/03/20/can-the-bloomberg -terminal-be-toppled/.

4. Barack Obama, Victory Speech at Grant Park in Chicago, Illinois (Nov. 4, 2008) (transcript available on CNN Politics website).

5. Michael Barbaro, "With Late Rush, Mayor Spent $102 Million on Election," *New York Times* (Nov. 28, 2009), A14.

6. Id.

7. Id.

8. "2020 Election to Cost $14 Billion, Blowing Away Spending Records," Center for Responsive Politics (Oct. 28, 2020, 1:51 PM), https://www.opensecrets .org/news/2020/10/cost-of-2020-election-14billion-update/.

9. *See* Brian Slodysko, "Bloomberg's Big Spending Struggles to Sway Election Outcomes," *AP News* (Nov. 14, 2020), https://apnews.com/article/election -2020-joe-biden-donald-trump-new-york-florida-69ea789b660ede5999388 be6edc615d6.

10. Adam Winkler, *We the Corporations: How American Businesses Won Their Civil Rights* (New York: Liveright, 2018), xv–xviii.

11. Philip Rucker, "Mitt Romney Says 'Corporations Are People,'" *Washington Post* (Aug. 11, 2011), https://www.washingtonpost.com/politics/mitt -romney-says-corporations-are-people/2011/08/11/gIQABwZ38I_story.html.

12. *Trustees of Dartmouth College v. Woodward*, 17 U.S. 518, 636 (1819).

13. *See Minneapolis & St. Louis Ry. Co. v. Beckwith*, 129 U.S. 26, 28 (1889); *Pembina Consol. Silver Mining & Milling Co. v. Commw. of Pa.*, 125 U.S. 181, 189 (1888).

14. *See*, for example, *FCC v. AT&T Inc.*, 562 U.S. 397, 409 (2011) (holding that corporations do not have "personal privacy" protections akin to those of natural persons); *First Nat'l Bank of Bos. v. Bellotti*, 435 U.S. 765, 784 (1978) (characterizing corporate political expenditures as speech protected under First Amendment); *Va. State Bd. of Pharmacy v. Va. Citizens Consumer Council, Inc.*, 425 U.S. 748, 770 (1976) (extending First Amendment protections to commercial speech); *New York Times Co. v. Sullivan*, 376 U.S. 254, 266 (1964) (affirming freedom of press to corporations); *NAACP v. Button*, 371 U.S. 415, 428–29 (1963) (recognizing free speech rights of nonprofit corporations); *NAACP v. Ala. ex rel. Patterson*, 357 U.S. 449, 460–62 (1958) (holding that nonprofit corporations possess freedom of speech); *Grosjean v. Am. Press Co.*, 297 U.S. 233, 244 (1936) (recognizing applicability of First Amendment's press protections to corporations); *Hale v. Henkel*, 201 U.S. 43, 71 (1906) (holding that corporations are protected by the Fourth Amendment against unreasonable searches and seizures); *Braswell v. United States*, 487 U.S. 99, 108–09 (1988) (holding that corporations do not enjoy Fifth Amendment protections).

15. *Citizens United v. FEC*, 558 U.S. 310, 343 (2010).

16. Mike McIntire and Nicholas Confessore, "Groups Shield Political Gifts of Businesses," *New York Times* (July 8, 2012), A1.

17. "Total Outside Spending by Election Cycle, All Groups," Center for Responsive Politics, https://www.opensecrets.org/outsidespending/cycle _tots.php?cycle=2016&view=A&chart=A#viewpt [https://perma.cc/M3TY -X3KD] (last visited Jan. 4, 2021) (reporting total spending on campaigns by noncandidates in various election cycles).

18. Id.

19. Id.

20. "2016 Outside Spending, by Super PAC," Center for Responsive Politics, https://www.opensecrets.org/outsidespending/summ.php?cycle =2016&chrt=V&disp=O&type=S (last visited Jan. 4, 2021).

21. "2020 Outside Spending, by Super PAC," Center for Responsive Politics, https://www.opensecrets.org/outsidespending/summ.php?cycle =2020&chrt=V&disp=O&type=S (last visited Jan. 4, 2021).

22. "Donor Demographics," Center for Responsive Politics, https://www .opensecrets.org/elections-overview/donor-demographics?cycle=2020& display=A (last visited Jan. 4, 2021).

23. Nicholas Confessore, Sarah Cohen, and Karen Yourish, "Just 158 Families Have Provided Nearly Half of the Early Money for Efforts to Capture the White House," *New York Times* (Oct. 10, 2015), https://www.nytimes.com/ interactive/2015/10/11/us/politics/2016-presidential-election-super-pac -donors.html.

24. Michael Beckel, *Issue One Outsized Influence Report* (2021), https://www .issueone.org/wp-content/uploads/2021/04/Issue-One-Outsized-Influence -Report-final.pdf.

25. *See* Ezra Klein, "The Most Depressing Graphic for Members of Congress," *Washington Post* (Jan. 14, 2013, 11:03 AM), https://www.washingtonpost .com/news/wonk/wp/2013/01/14/the-most-depressing-graphic-for -members-of-congress/.

26. *Burwell v. Hobby Lobby Stores, Inc.*, 573 U.S. 682, 720 (2014).

27. 42 U.S.C. § 2000bb–1(a) (1993).

28. *Burwell v. Hobby Lobby Stores*, 711–12.

Chapter 4

1. ALS Facts and Statistics, *ALS News Today*, https://alsnewstoday.com/als -facts-statistics/ (last visited Jan. 4, 2021).

2. "Ice Bucket Challenge Co-Creator Patrick Quinn Dies Aged 37," *Guardian*, https://www.theguardian.com/us-news/2020/nov/23/ice-bucket-challenge -co-creator-patrick-quinn-dies-aged-37 (last updated Nov. 23, 2020).

3. Simon Mainwaring, *We First: How Brands and Consumers Use Social Media to Build a Better World* (London: Palgrave Macmillan, 2011), 6.

4. Jeremy Heimans and Henry Timms, *New Power: How Power Works in Our Hyperconnected World—and How to Make It Work for You* (New York: Doubleday, 2019), 2.

5. Farhad Manjoo, "How Battling Brands Online Has Gained Urgency, and Impact," *New York Times* (June 22, 2017), B7.

6. Public Facilities Privacy & Security Act, 2016 N.C. Sess. Laws 12, *repealed by* Act to Reset S.L. 2016-3, 2017 N.C. Sess. Laws 81.

7. Dave Philipps, "North Carolina Limits Bathroom Use by Birth Gender," *New York Times* (Mar. 24, 2016), A15.

8. Richard Fausset and Alan Blinder, "Bias Law Deepens Rifts in North Carolina," *New York Times* (Apr. 12, 2016), A12.

9. "NCAA to Relocate Championships from North Carolina for 2016–17," press release, National Collegiate Athletic Association (Sept. 12, 2016, 6:10 PM).

10. Human Rights Campaign, "More Than 100 Major CEOs & Business Leaders Urge North Carolina To Repeal Anti-LGBT Law," letter from business leaders to Pat McCrory, Governor of North Carolina, March 31, 2016, https://www .hrc.org/press-releases/more-than-100-major-ceos-business-leaders-demand -north-carolina-repeal-radi.

11. Emery P. Dalesio and Jonathan Drew, "AP Exclusive: Price Tag of North Carolina's LGBT Law: $3.76B," *AP News* (Mar. 27, 2017), https://apnews.com/ article/fa4528580f3e4a01bb68bcb272f1f0f8.

12. *See* Kurt Badenhausen, "The World's Most Valuable Sports Teams 2020," *Forbes* (July 31, 2020, 6:30 AM), https://www.forbes.com/sites /kurtbadenhausen/2020/07/31/the-worlds-most-valuable-sports -teams-2020/?sh=7068d1c83c74.

13. Neil Vigdor, "FedEx Joins Push for Washington Redskins to Be Renamed," *New York Times* (July 16, 2020), https://www.nytimes.com/2020/07/02/ sports/Redskins-name-FedEx.html.

14. John Keim, "How the Events of 2020 Have Changed the Washington Football Team," *ESPN* (Aug. 20, 2020), https://www.espn.com/nfl/story/_/ id/29460299/how-events-2020-changed-washington-football-team.

15. *See* Scott McDonald, "Washington Redskins Urged to Lose Name, or Millions in Sponsorships," *Newsweek* (July 1, 2020, 8:26 PM), https:// www.newsweek.com/washington-redskins-urged-lose-name-millions -sponsorships-1514894.

16. *See* Keim, "How the Events of 2020."

17. Vigdor, "FedEx Joins Push."

18. Terry M. Neal, "McCain Reverses Flag Stance," *Washington Post* (Apr. 20, 2000), https://www.washingtonpost.com/archive/politics/2000/04/20/ mccain-reverses-flag-stance/2127f2a1-553b-4cc8-a587-f3324547069c/.

19. Greta Thunberg, *No One Is Too Small to Make a Difference* (London: Penguin, 2019).

Chapter 5

1. Alexandra Alter, "Still Too Plausible for Comfort," *New York Times* (Nov. 10, 2018), C1.

2. *Federalist*, no. 51 (New York: New York Packet).

3. *See* Daryl J. Levinson and Richard H. Pildes, "Separation of Parties, Not Powers," *Harvard Law Review* 119 (2006): 2311.

4. Ezra Klein, *Why We're Polarized* (New York: Avid Reader Press, 2020), 136–37.

5. Ezra Klein, "Congressional Dysfunction," *Vox*, https://www.vox.com/2015/1/2/18089154/congressional-dysfunction (last updated May 15, 2015, 6:18 PM).

6. "Here's Donald Trump's Presidential Announcement Speech," *Time* (June 16, 2015, 2:32 PM), https://time.com/3923128/donald-trump-announcement -speech/.

7. Edelman Trust Barometer 20201, https://www.edelman.com/trust/2021 -trust-barometer.

8. Jenna Johnson, "Trump Calls For 'Total and Complete Shutdown of Muslims Entering the United States,'" *Washington Post* (Dec. 7, 2015, 8:12 PM), https://www.washingtonpost.com/news/post-politics/wp/2015/12/07/donald-trump -calls-for-total-and-complete-shutdown-of-muslims-entering-the-united -states/.

9. Besheer Mohamed, "New Estimates Show U.S. Muslim Population Continues to Grow," Pew Research Center (Jan. 3, 2018), https://www.pewresearch .org/fact-tank/2018/01/03/new-estimates-show-u-s-muslim-population -continues-to-grow/.

10. Alia E. Dastagir, "Outrage Over Trump's Immigrant Ban Helps ACLU Raise More Money Online in One Weekend Than in All of 2016," *USA Today* (Jan. 30, 2017, 3:43 PM), https://www.usatoday.com/story/news/nation/2017/01/29/aclu-fundraising-records-muslim-immigrant-ban/97218098/.

11. Mike Isaac, "What You Need to Know About #DeleteUber," *New York Times* (Jan. 31, 2017), https://www.nytimes.com/2017/01/31/business/delete-uber .html.

12. T. C. Sottek, "Netflix CEO: 'Trump's Actions Are So Un-American It Pains Us All,'" *Verge* (Jan. 28, 2017, 5:14 PM), https://www.theverge.com/2017/1/28/14426536/netflix-reed-hastings-trump-immigration-executive -order.

13. Letter from Howard Schultz, chairman and CEO, Starbucks, to Starbucks Partners, on Living Our Values in Uncertain Times (Jan. 29, 2017) (on file with the Starbucks website).

14. Joe Heim et al., "Charlottesville Protest Takes a Deadly Turn," *Washington Post* (Aug. 13, 2017), A14.

15. Glenn Thrush and Maggie Haberman, "Critics Slam Trump's Tepid Condemnation of Violence on 'Many Sides' in Virginia," *New York Times* (Aug. 13, 2017), A14.

16. Angie Drobnic Holan, "In Context: Donald Trump's 'Very Fine People on Both Sides' Remarks" (transcript), *PolitiFact* (Apr. 26, 2019), https://www .politifact.com/article/2019/apr/26/context-trumps-very-fine-people-both -sides-remarks/.

17. Jacob Pramuk, "Trump Administration Ending DACA Program, Which Protected 800,000 Children of Immigrants," *CNBC* (Sept. 5, 2017, 9:05 PM), https://www.cnbc.com/2017/09/05/trump-administration-is-ending-daca -immigration-program-ag-sessions-says.html.

18. Attorney Gen. Jeff Sessions, Remarks Discussing the Immigration Enforcement Actions of the Trump Administration (May 7, 2018) (transcript available with the U.S. Department of Justice).

19. Philip Bump, "Trump's 'Deterrent' of Separating Kids from Their Parents Isn't Deterring Many Migrants," *Washington Post* (June 7, 2018, 3:14 PM), https:// www.washingtonpost.com/news/politics/wp/2018/06/07/trumps-deterrent -of-separating-kids-from-their-parents-doesnt-even-seem-to-work/.

20. Eli Rosenberg, "Sessions Defends Separating Immigrant Parents and Children: 'We've Got to Get This Message Out,'" *Washington Post* (June 5, 2018, 10:28 PM), https://www.washingtonpost.com/news/post-politics/ wp/2018/06/05/sessions-defends-separating-immigrant-parents-and -children-weve-got-to-get-this-message-out/.

21. Zach Wichter, "C.E.O.s See a 'Sad Day' After Trump's DACA Decision," *New York Times* (Sept. 5, 2017), https://www.nytimes.com/2017/09/05/business/ chief-executives-see-a-sad-day-after-trumps-daca-decision.html.

Chapter 6

1. "US Government Lists Fictional Nation Wakanda as Trade Partner," *BBC News* (Dec. 19, 2019), https://www.bbc.com/news/world-us-canada -50849559.

2. Scott Ellsworth, *Tulsa Race Massacre*, Oklahoma Historical Society, https:// www.okhistory.org/publications/enc/entry.php?entry=TU013. (last visited Feb. 25, 2021).

3. Id.

4. President Barack Obama, Race Speech at the Constitution Center: A More Perfect Union (Mar. 18, 2008).

5. Haley Willis et al., "New Footage Shows Delayed Medical Response to George Floyd," *New York Times* (Aug. 11, 2020), https://www.nytimes.com/2020/08/11/us/george-floyd-body-cam-full-video.html.

6. Michael J. de la Merced, "Netflix Moving $100 Million to Empower Black Banks," *New York Times* (July 1, 2020), B4.

7. Jessica Bursztynsky, "JPMorgan Chase Announces Latest Efforts in Its $30 Billion Commitment to Address Racial Inequality," *CNBC* (Feb. 23, 2021, 11:54 AM), https://www.cnbc.com/2021/02/23/jpmorgans-announces-efforts-in-its-commitment-to-help close-racial-wealth-gap.html.

8. JPMorgan Chase, "JPMorgan Chase Announces Initiatives to Support Minority-Owned and Diverse-Led Financial Institutions," *Cision* (Feb. 23, 2021, 7:58 AM), https://www.prnewswire.com/news-releases/jpmorgan-chase-announces-initiatives-to-support-minority-owned-and-diverse-led-financial-institutions-301233393.html.

9. Mehrsa Baradaran, *The Color of Money: Black Banks and the Racial Wealth Gap* (Cambridge: Belknap Press of Harvard University Press, 2017), 2.

10. Otis Rolley, "Dr. Martin Luther King, Jr. and His Push for Economic Justice," Rockefeller Foundation (Jan. 15, 2021), https://www.rockefellerfoundation.org/blog/martin-luther-king-jr-and-his-push-for-economic-justice/.

11. Id.

12. Id.

13. Bryan Hancock et al., "Race in the Workplace: The Black Experience in the US Private Sector," *McKinsey* (Feb. 21, 2021), https://www.mckinsey.com/featured-insights/diversity-and-inclusion/Race-in-the-workplace-The-Black-experience-in-the-US-private-sector.

14. Id.

15. Martin Luther King, Jr., "All Labor Has Dignity," speech at Bishop Charles Mason Temple of the Church of God in Christ (Mar. 18, 1968) (transcript available on Beacon Broadside website).

16. *See* World Econ. Forum, *The Global Gender Gap Report* 9 (2018).

17. Ibid.

18. Kate Whiting, "7 Surprising and Outrageous Stats About Gender Inequality," *World Economic Forum* (Mar. 8, 2019), https://www.weforum.org/agenda/2019/03/surprising-stats-about-gender-inequality/.

19. Id.

20. "16 Shocking Facts About Gender Inequality," Pan Macmillan (June 16, 2020), https://www.panmacmillan.com/blogs/lifestyle-wellbeing/shocking-gender-inequality-facts-melinda-gates.

21 Id.

22. Id.

23. "Fast Facts: The Gender Pay Gap," American Association of University Women, https://www.aauw.org/resources/article/fast-facts-pay-gap/ (last visited Feb. 25, 2021).

24. Kimberly Churches, "Why the Pay Gap Persists in High-Paying Professions," American Association of University Women (Oct. 20, 2019), https://www.aauw.org/resources/news/media/insights/why-the-pay-gap-persists-in-high-paying-professions/.

25. Id.

26. "More Than 12M 'Me Too' Facebook Posts, Comments, Reactions, in 24 Hours," *CBS News* (Oct. 17, 2017, 6:26 PM), https://www.cbsnews.com/news/metoo-more-than-12-million-facebook-posts-comments-reactions-24-hours/.

27. Vivian Hunt, Sara Prince, Sundiatu Dixon-Fyle, and Lareina Yee, *Delivering Through Diversity*, McKinsey (Jan. 2018), https://www.mckinsey.com/~/media/mckinsey/business%20functions/organization/our%20insights/delivering%20through%20diversity/delivering-through-diversity_full-report.ashx.

28. Stephen Turban, Dan Wu, and Letian Zhang, "Research: When Gender Diversity Makes Firms More Productive," *Harvard Business Review* (Feb. 11, 2019), https://hbr.org/2019/02/research-when-gender-diversity-makes-firms-more-productive.

29. "COVID-19 Cost Women Globally Over $800 Billion in Lost Income in One Year," press release, Oxfam International (Apr. 29, 2021), https://www.oxfam.org/en/press-releases/covid-19-cost-women-globally-over-800-billion-lost-income-one-year.

30. Melinda Gates, *The Moment of Lift: How Empowering Women Changes the World* (New York: Flatiron Books, 2019), 27.

31. Id.

32. Seema Mody, "Diversity Drives Profits, But It Is Still Lacking in the Board Room," CNBC (June 12, 2020, 2:52 PM), https://www.cnbc.com/2020/06/12/diversity-drives-profits-but-it-is-still-lacking-in-the-board-room.html.

33. *See* Paul Gompers and Silpa Kovvali, "The Other Diversity Dividend," *Harvard Business Review* (July-Aug. 2018): 72–77; Stephen Turban, Dan Wu, and Letian Zhang, "Research: When Gender Diversity Makes Firms More Productive," *Harvard Business Review* (Feb. 11, 2019), https://hbr.org/2019/02/research-when-gender-diversity-makes-firms-more-productive; "Appendix: Why Diversity and Inclusion Matter: Financial Performance," *Catalyst* (June 24, 2020), https://www.catalyst.org/research/why-diversity-and-inclusion-matter-financial-performance/.

34. President Lyndon B. Johnson, Commencement Address at Howard University: "To Fulfill These Rights" (June 4, 1965), https://teachingamericanhistory.org/library/document/commencement-address-at-howard-university-to-fulfill-these-rights/.

Chapter 7

1. Geoff Edgers, *Walk This Way: Run-DMC, Aerosmith, and the Song That Changed American Music Forever* (New York: Penguin Random House, 2019), 9–10.

2. Id.

3. Gates Foundation, "Who We Are: Foundation Fact Sheet," https://www.gatesfoundation.org/who-we-are/general-information/foundation-factsheet (last visited Feb. 9, 2021).

4. Id.

5. Sarah Boseley, "How Bill and Melinda Gates Helped Save 122M Lives—And What They Want to Solve Next," *Guardian* (Feb. 14, 2017, 5:00 PM), https://www.theguardian.com/world/2017/feb/14/bill-gates-philanthropy-warren-buffett-vaccines-infant-mortality.

6. Bill and Melinda Gates, "Warren Buffet's Best Investment," *GatesNotes* (Feb. 14, 2017), https://www.gatesnotes.com/2017-Annual-Letter?WT.mc_id=02_14_2017_02_OutreachEmail_IN-GFO_&WT.tsrc=INGFO.

7. Id.

8. Tim Cook, "Pro-Discrimination 'Religious Freedom' Laws Are Dangerous," *Washington Post* (Mar. 29, 2015), https://www.washingtonpost.com/opinions/pro-discrimination-religious-freedom-laws-are-dangerous-to-america/2015/03/29/bdb4ce9e-d66d-11e4-ba28-f2a685dc7f89_story.html.

9. "Advance Your NGO's Mission," Western Union, https://business.westernunion.com/en-us/global-payment-solutions/ngo (last visited Feb. 9, 2021).

10. April Jordin, "Project Last Mile Initiative Continues to Expand in Africa," Coca-Cola Journey (Jan. 19, 2016) (describing collaboration between Coca-Cola and nonprofit partners, including Gates Foundation).

11. *See* Matthew Bishop and Michael Green, "Philanthrocapitalism: How the Rich Can Save the World" (London: Bloomsbury Publishing, 2008), 2–3; Bill Gates, Co-Chair and Tr., Gates Foundation, prepared remarks at the 2008 World Economic Forum—Creative Capitalism (Jan. 24, 2008) (transcript available on Gates Foundation website).

12. Minow, *Partners, Not Rivals*, 6.

13. "Our Mission," Emerson Collective, https://www.emersoncollective.com/about-us/ (last visited Feb. 9, 2021).

14. Charlie LeDuff, *Detroit: An American Autopsy* (London: Penguin, 2014), 4.

15. *Five Years After JPMorgan Chase's $150 Million Investment in Detroit*, JPMorgan Chase, https://www.jpmorganchase.com/news-stories/committed -to-detroits-future (last visited Feb. 9, 2021).

16. Id.

17. Matthew Heimer, "How JPMorgan Chase is Fueling Detroit's Revival," *Fortune* (Sept. 7, 2017, 6:30 AM), https://fortune.com/2017/09/07/jp -morgan-chase-detroit-revival/.

18. Id.

19. Id.

20. Federal Reserve Bank of Chicago, *Detroit Economic Activity Index (DEAI)*, https://www.chicagofed.org/publications/deai/index (last updated Dec. 3, 2020).

21. "What Are Levi's WaterLess Jeans?," giving fashion (Aug. 3, 2018), https:// www.givingfashion.com/new-blog/2018/8/3/what-are-levis-waterless-jeans; "How We Make Jeans with Less Water," Levi's (March 2018), https://www .levi.com/US/en_US/blog/article/how-we-make-jeans-with-less-water/.

22. Fred Krupp, 'Walmart: The Awakening of an Environmental Giant," *Huffington Post* (Dec. 6, 2017), http://www.huffingtonpost.com/fred-krupp/ walmart-the-awakening-of_b_9253920.html; "Sustainability," Walmart, http://corporate.walmart.com/global-responsibility/sustainability/ (last visited Feb. 9, 2021).

23. "Buy a Pair, Give a Pair: The Whole Story Begins with You," Warby Parker, https://www.warbyparker.com/buy-a-pair-give-a-pair (last visited Feb. 9, 2021).

24. 2019 Edelman Trust Barometer Special Report: Institutional Investors, https://cdn2.hubspot.net/hubfs/440941/Edelman%20Trust%20Special% 20Report%20II.pdf.

25. *See* Siobhan Riding, "Majority of ESG Funds Outperform Wider Market Over 10 Years," *Financial Times* (June 13, 2020), https://www.ft.com/ content/733ee6ff-446e-4f8b-86b2-19ef42da3824; John Mackey and Raj Sisodia, *Conscious Capitalism* (Brighton: Harvard Business Review Press, 2014), 276–83; Shuili Du, C.B. Bhattacharya, and Sankar Sen, "Maximizing Business Returns to Corporate Social Responsibility (CSR): The Role of CSR Communication," *International* Journal of Management *Reviews* 12(1) (2010): 8, 9.

26. *See* MSCI ESG Research LLC, "Swipe to Invest: The Story Behind Millennials and ESG Investing" (March 2020), https://www.msci.com/documents/ 10199/07e7a7d3-59c3-4d0b-b0b5-029e8fd3974b; EY, "Sustainable Investing: The Millennial Investor (2017)," https://assets.ey.com/content/dam/ey-sites/ ey-com/en_gl/topics/financial-services/ey-sustainable-investing-the -millennial-investor.pdf.

27. Jill Cornfield, "Millennials Look to Make a Social Impact with Their Investing Dollar, Study Finds," *CNBC* (July 15, 2020, 7:40 AM), https://www.cnbc.com/2020/07/14/millennials-look-to-make-a-social-impact-with-their-investing-dollar.html.

28. Debbie Carlson, "ESG Investing Now Accounts for One-Third of Total U.S. Assets Under Management," *MarketWatch* (Nov. 17, 2020, 10:23 AM), https://www.marketwatch.com/story/esg-investing-now-accounts-for-one-third-of-total-u-s-assets-under-management-11605626611.

Chapter 8

1. Artemis Moshtaghian and Rebekah Riess, "Suspect Indicted in Fatal Stabbing at Maryland Popeyes After Argument," *CNN* (Dec. 17, 2019, 6:01 PM), https://www.cnn.com/2019/12/17/us/popeyes-sandwich-stabbing-suspect-indicted/index.html.

2. Rebekah Schouten, "Slideshow: The Chicken Sandwich Wars Rage On," *Food Business News* (Jan. 13, 2021), https://www.foodbusinessnews.net/articles/17685-slideshow-the-chicken-sandwich-wars-rage-on.

3. "Who We Are," Chick-fil-A, https://www.chick-fil-a.com/about/who-we-are (last visited Feb. 10, 2021).

4. "Giving Back," Chick-fil-A, https://www.chick-fil-a.com/about/giving-back (last visited Feb. 10, 2021).

5. Myles Collier, "Chick-fil-A President Says 'God's Judgment' Coming Because of Same-Sex Marriage," *Christian Post* (July 18, 2012), https://www.christianpost.com/news/chick-fil-a-president-says-gods-judgment-coming-because-of-same-sex-marriage-78485/#SUuZKIURo5MhCW2p.99.

6. "Chick-fil-A, Chick-fil-A Response to Recent Controversy," press release, Chick-fil-A (2012), https://web.archive.org/web/20121012171028/http://www.chick-fil-a.com/Media/PDF/LGBT-statement.pdf.

7. Richard Fausset, "Delta Took a Stand on the N.R.A.; Georgia Lawmakers Want to Make It Pay," *New York Times* (March 2, 2018), A12.

8. Antonia Noori Farzan, "A Mexican Restaurant is Facing Backlash After Saying It Was an 'Honor' to Serve Jeff Sessions," *Washington Post* (Aug. 13, 2018, 6:12 AM), https://www.washingtonpost.com/news/morning-mix/wp/2018/08/13/a-mexican-restaurant-is-facing-backlash-after-saying-it-was-an-honor-to-serve-jeff-sessions/.

9. Id.

10. Deloitte, "Missing Pieces Report: The 2018 Board Diversity Census of Women and Minorities on Fortune 500 Boards" (2019), 17, https://www2.deloitte.com/us/en/pages/center-for-board-effectiveness/articles/missing-pieces-fortune-500-board-diversity-study-2018.html.

11. Id.

12. Michael J. Sandel, *What Money Can't Buy: The Moral Limits of Markets* (New York: Farrar, Straus and Giroux, 2013), 130.

13. Mitch Landrieu, *In the Shadow of Statues: A White Southerner Confronts History* (London: Penguin, 2018), 126.

14. Joel Bakan, *The Corporation: The Pathological Pursuit of Profit and Power* (New York: Free Press, 2005), 88.

15. Edwin Black, *IBM and the Holocaust: The Strategic Alliance Between Nazi Germany and America's Most Powerful Corporation* (New York: Crown, 2001).

16. *See Citizens United v. FEC*, 558 U.S. 310, 361–62 (2010).

17. Melissa J. Durkee, "Astroturf Activism," *Stanford Law Review* 69 (2017): 201, 229.

18. Anand Giridharadas, *Winners Take All: The Elite Charade of Changing the World* (New York: Vintage Books, 2019), 8–9.

Chapter 9

1. "This Bizarre Secret About Ben & Jerry's Co-Founder Nearly Meant That the Business Never Existed," Twisted Food (May 17, 2018), https://twistedfood .co.uk/this-bizarre-secret-about-ben-jerrys-co-founder-nearly-meant-that -the-business-never-existed.

2. "Our Values," Ben & Jerry's, https://www.benjerry.com/values (last visited Feb. 19, 2021).

3. David Gelles, "Gobbled Up, But Still Doing Good for the World," *New York Times* (Aug. 21, 2015), BU3.

4. "Sustainable Living," Unilever, https://www.unilever.co.uk/sustainable-living/ (last visited Feb. 19, 2021).

5. "Ten Years of Sustainable Living Achievements," Unilever, https://www .unilever.co.uk/sustainable-living/ten-years-of-sustainable-living -achievement.html (last visited Feb. 19, 2021).

6. Thomas Buckley, "Unilever Wants to Give Mayo and Marmite a Purpose," *Bloomberg Businessweek* (Aug. 15, 2019, 8:49 AM), https://www.bloomberg .com/news/articles/2019-08-15/unilever-wants-to-give-mayo-and-marmite -a-purpose.

7. "Every Dove Teaches Girls Self-Esteem," Unilever, https://www.unilever.com/ about/every-u-does-good/dove/ (last visited Feb. 19., 2021).

8. Liam Stack, "Yemenis Shut Stores and Hold Rally to Protest Trump Ban," *New York Times* (Feb. 3, 2017), A22.

9. Matt Stevens, "C.E.O. Apologizes After the Arrests of 2 Black Men Sitting at Starbucks," *New York Times* (Apr. 16, 2018), B5.

Chapter 10

1. Letter from Larry Fink, CEO of BlackRock, to CEOs (2021) (on file with BlackRock).

2. Daniel H. Pink, *Drive: The Surprising Truth About What Motivates Us* (New York: Penguin, 2011), 132–33.

3. *See* Justin Fox and Jay W. Lorsch, "What Good Are Shareholders?," *Harvard Business Review* (July–Aug. 2012): 48, 57; Jim Stengel, *Grow: How Ideals Power Growth and Profit at the World's Greatest Companies* (New York: Crown, 2011), 1–2, 22–33; George Serafeim and Claudine Gartenberg, "The Type of Purpose That Makes Companies More Profitable," *Harvard Business Review* (Oct. 21, 2016), https://hbr.org/2016/10/the-type-of-purpose-that-makes-companies-more-profitable.

4. The 2020 Axios Harris 100 Corporate Reputation Rankings, https://theharrispoll.com/wp-content/uploads/2020/07/HP-RQ-2020-v9-1.pdf.

5. "Who We Are: Foundation Fact Sheet," Gates Foundation, https://www.gatesfoundation.org/Who-We-Are/General-Information/Foundation-Factsheet (last visited Feb. 19, 2021).

6. William Bruce Cameron, *Informal Sociology: A Casual Introduction to Sociological Thinking* (New York: Random House, 1963), 13.

Conclusion

1. Kurt Badenhausen, "Michael Jordan Has Made Over $1 Billion from Nike—The Biggest Endorsement Bargain In Sports," *Forbes* (May 3, 2020, 10:06 AM), https://www.forbes.com/sites/kurtbadenhausen/2020/05/03/michael-jordans-1-billion-nike-endorsement-is-the-biggest-bargain-in-sports/?sh=1e4363cc6136.

2. "#9 LeBron James," *Forbes* (June 4, 2020), https://www.forbes.com/profile/lebron-james/?sh=3ef2a0802398.

3. Sean Gregory, "*Time* Athlete of the Year: LeBron James," *Time* (Dec. 10, 2020), https://time.com/athlete-of-the-year-2020-lebron-james/.

ACKNOWLEDGMENTS

E VERY BOOK CONTAINS AT LEAST TWO STORIES: the story itself and the story of the storyteller, for each story is forged by the tale of its teller. For this book, neither of those stories are self-made. Luck played an important role, as did the work, generosity, grace, and kindness of others. Much gratitude is owed.

Thanks to Steve Piersanti, Jeevan Sivasubramaniam, Michael Crowley, Valerie Caldwell, and the rest of the team at Berrett-Koehler for all of their hard work in connection with the book.

This book benefited immeasurably from the scholarship, writings, insights, indulgence, time, and expertise that others were so generous in sharing with me directly for the book, and in the years prior with the research and writing that served as the building blocks of the book. There are too many to enumerate in their entirety, but I want to especially thank Mehrsa Baradaran, Jonah Berger, Robert Cialdini, Lawrence Cunningham, James Fanto, Jill Fisch, Joan Heminway, Kristin Johnson, Donald Langevoort,

Martin Lipton, Andrew C.W. Lund, Martha Minow, Elizabeth Pollman, Jeff Schwartz, Megan Shaner, Omari Scott Simmons, Lynn Stout, and Leo E. Strine, Jr., as well as numerous business executives, entrepreneurs, organizational leaders, and lawyers who shared their experiences and views in confidence.

The core ideas of this book drew and built upon much of my previous research and writings, in particular two law review articles: "Incorporating Social Activism" in the *Boston University Law Review* and "Executive Private Misconduct" in the *George Washington Law Review*. I am grateful to the staff and editors of both law reviews for their diligence and efforts, which helped me refine my writing and ideas for this book.

Some of the questions and ideas embedded in the book were prompted and developed from exchanges and discussions with numerous students over the years. I am grateful to them for pushing me to rethink the world and the law as it is, and to think more about what they could and ought to be.

The writing of the book and its underlying research in prior years was enhanced by the assistance of a number of hardworking and talented researchers, readers, and editors. I want to especially thank Anjali Deshpande, Kelly Duffner, Kristi Hein, Thomas Helbig, Eleanor Bradley Huyett, Noa Kaumeheiwa, Emily Litka, Leslie Minora, Kevin Rajan, Matthew Sherman, George Tsoflias, and the staff of the Temple Law Library.

I have been fortunate to call Temple University School of Law my professional home. This book and the writings leading up to it have benefited from this affiliation, as well as the efforts, insights, and graciousness of my colleagues and administrators—past and present—in ways large and small. In particular, I want thank Alice Abreu, Jennifer Bretschneider, Michelle Cosby, Jeffrey Dunoff, JoAnne Epps, Donald Harris, Duncan

Hollis, Ken Jacobsen, Jonathan Lipson, Gregory Mandel, Jaya Ramji-Nogales, Rachel Rebouche, and Harwell Wells.

My worldview on matters of life, business, law, and society has been shaped and reshaped by numerous good friends, some of whom I have already acknowledged here. I want to thank them (again), in particular those who have served as my brain trust, for their profound friendships, candid views, and insightful wit.

Finally, I am grateful for my family, near and far, for making my story possible, meaningful, and wonderful in more ways than I truly deserve.

INDEX

ABOUT THE AUTHOR

TOM C.W. LIN is an award-winning law professor at Temple University's Beasley School of Law. He is also an Academic Fellow at George Washington University's Center for Law, Economics & Finance. He teaches and writes in the areas of business organizations, corporate governance, and financial regulation. His research  and scholarship have been published in many leading academic law journals and cited by courts and regulatory bodies around the world. His expertise has also been featured in major media outlets like *Bloomberg News*, *CNN*, *Fortune*, the *Financial Times*, the *Wall Street Journal*, and the *Washington Post*.

Berrett–Koehler
Publishers

Berrett-Koehler is an independent publisher dedicated to an ambitious mission: *Connecting people and ideas to create a world that works for all.*

Our publications span many formats, including print, digital, audio, and video. We also offer online resources, training, and gatherings. And we will continue expanding our products and services to advance our mission.

We believe that the solutions to the world's problems will come from all of us, working at all levels: in our society, in our organizations, and in our own lives. Our publications and resources offer pathways to creating a more just, equitable, and sustainable society. They help people make their organizations more humane, democratic, diverse, and effective (and we don't think there's any contradiction there). And they guide people in creating positive change in their own lives and aligning their personal practices with their aspirations for a better world.

And we strive to practice what we preach through what we call "The BK Way." At the core of this approach is *stewardship,* a deep sense of responsibility to administer the company for the benefit of all of our stakeholder groups, including authors, customers, employees, investors, service providers, sales partners, and the communities and environment around us. Everything we do is built around stewardship and our other core values of *quality, partnership, inclusion,* and *sustainability.*

This is why Berrett-Koehler is the first book publishing company to be both a B Corporation (a rigorous certification) and a benefit corporation (a for-profit legal status), which together require us to adhere to the highest standards for corporate, social, and environmental performance. And it is why we have instituted many pioneering practices (which you can learn about at www.bkconnection.com), including the Berrett-Koehler Constitution, the Bill of Rights and Responsibilities for BK Authors, and our unique Author Days.

We are grateful to our readers, authors, and other friends who are supporting our mission. We ask you to share with us examples of how BK publications and resources are making a difference in your lives, organizations, and communities at www.bkconnection.com/impact.

Dear reader,

Thank you for picking up this book and welcome to the worldwide BK community! You're joining a special group of people who have come together to create positive change in their lives, organizations, and communities.

What's BK all about?

Our mission is to connect people and ideas to create a world that works for all.

Why? Our communities, organizations, and lives get bogged down by old paradigms of self-interest, exclusion, hierarchy, and privilege. But we believe that can change. That's why we seek the leading experts on these challenges—and share their actionable ideas with you.

A welcome gift

To help you get started, we'd like to offer you a **free copy** of one of our bestselling ebooks:

www.bkconnection.com/welcome

When you claim your **free ebook**, you'll also be subscribed to our blog.

Our freshest insights

Access the best new tools and ideas for leaders at all levels on our blog at ideas.bkconnection.com.

Sincerely,

Your friends at Berrett-Koehler